Virtues in Verse

THE BEST OF BERTON BRALEY

VIRTUES IN VERSE: THE BEST OF BERTON BRALEY

Selected and Arranged by Linda Tania Abrams

Cover Design and Illustration by Stephen Klopfstein

Published by
The Atlantean Press
Milpitas, California

Printed in the United States of America

ISBN 0-9626854-3-7
LC 93-73134

Virtues in Verse

THE BEST OF BERTON BRALEY

Selected and Arranged by Linda Tania Abrams

The Atlantean Press

This sketch of Berton Braley, signed "C Sutherland," was found in Braley's scrapbook, labelled "Honolulu 1923." The verse reads:

> A man who writes poems & verses & rhyme
> And sells 'em, by gum, in his leisurely time
> And sees almost always a happier way
> To be a good fellow and make living pay—
> An artist with words, a sculptor with meter
> With a healthy philosophy—(what could be sweeter?)

(Published with permission of Ian Braley.)

CONTENTS

Virtues Inverse: New Deal Ditties

People & Places

Lovers & Lasses

Potpourri

Excerpts from *Pegasus Pulls a Hack: Memoirs of a Modern Minstrel*

Postscript

"... unquestionably the most widely read American poet of today ..."
—Honolulu *Star-Bulletin*, 1923

"Berton Braley is the most prolific verse writer in America today, with the additional boast that all of his verse rhymes."
—Brooklyn *Eagle*, circa 1936

"Berton Braley ... is perhaps the leading humorous poet in America to-day.... There is no magazine of any consequence in the country that has not bought poetry from Berton Braley."—Brooklyn *Citizen*, 1912

"Berton Braley is continually running the risk of being held before schoolboys as 'the American Kipling' ... He is doing for ... workers generally what Kipling did for the British soldier."—*Human Life*, 1910

"... let anyone say 'Berton Braley,' in the average crowd of regular Americans and it's dollars to doughnuts that he'll poll a larger number of hands than any of the well known old masters that we learned about in 'History of English Literature,' in high school.... a poet who is endeared to the people, and who is a perfect craftsman and sure of his art."
—[a Portland, Oregon newspaper, circa 1919]

"... the life and spirit and vigor and fire of youth is in his work, and that is what make his 'stuff,' as he is pleased to designate the product of his facile typewriter, so popular."—Charleston *News*, 1913

"... even the most Philistine American can't help quoting his lines ..."
—Buffalo *Evening News*, 1915

"... The reader will here find poems for every occasion and every mood, poems of inspiration, humor and adventure, poems of work and play—a great variety of subjects all treated in Berton Braley's best manner."
—Utica, New York *Press*, 1927

"... certainly you will be hard to please and of a strange occupation if you do not find something to your taste in these robust rhymes."
—*San Francisco Chronicle*, 1915

" 'Songs of the Workaday World' ... is a part of the great Illiad of labor and embodies the sturdy ideals that some persons have feared were vanishing from our literature and from our national life."
—*Review of Reviews*, January 1, 1916

"... sometimes called the Kipling of the Masses ..."
—Springfield, Massachusetts *News*, 1915

"He is a versifier of the first class ... Berton Braley's verse today is as ubiquitous as a Ford car. And like a Ford car, it gets places ..."
—*New York Times Sunday Review*, 1934

Editor's Introduction

Berton Braley, sometimes called "the American Kipling" and "the Bard of Business and the Merry Minstrel of Mechanics," was a popular and immensely prolific poet during the first half of this century. How did he earn those monikers? And why have we titled this compilation of his work "Virtues in Verse"?

Berton Braley (1882-1966) was born and raised in Madison, Wisconsin and graduated from the University of Wisconsin in 1905. At eighteen, he decided to be a writer; until then he had sold only one poem, but during his college years his verses began to appear in the school paper, and he self-published two little compilations.

From a variety of summer and part-time jobs held in those years, and from his first job after college—as a reporter in Butte, Montana—Braley began to acquire his knowledge of the "working world," of "life as the other man lives it," that would eventually lead to his first major book of poems in 1915, *Songs of the Workaday World*. Those jobs ranged from freighter deckhand to bookseller, from miner to asylum gardener. But from 1909, when he sold a group of ten "Mining Camp Ballads" to the *Saturday Evening Post* and set out for New York City, he built a reputation and career as a full-time, freelance, professional "versifier" and writer.

Braley traces his literary development in his book *Pegasus Pulls a Hack: Memoirs of a Modern Minstrel* (1934), excerpts from which are included at the end of this compilation. There, in his own words, he describes the circumstances and the conscious judgments, insights, and attitudes that led to his unique role as "the Machine Age Poet," "the Bard of Business and the Merry Minstrel of Mechanics": the staff poet of *Coal Age, American Machinist, Power,* and the *Engineering Journal,* and frequent contributor to the *Nation's Business, Forbes Magazine, Harper's, The Century, Atlantic Monthly, Iron Age,* the *Saturday Evening Post,* and nearly every major popular magazine of his day.

Braley was extraordinarily prolific: his *New York Times* obituary (1/27/66) credits him with "verses by the thousands, short stories by the hundreds and books by the score." Judging from the quantity and tenor of his press clippings, he was clearly one of America's most popular versifiers. Of his more than 20 books, at least 10 are poetry.

His work appeared in almost every medium possible: in the big magazines as well as the "pulps," in newspaper syndicates and industry journals, in advertisements and greeting cards. For three years he wrote a newspaper column, "Berton Braley's Daily Poem," regularly syndicated by the Newspaper Enterprise Association (N.E.A.) to 60 to 70 daily papers. Other sources credit him with 9,000 to 12,000 *published* poems and 300 short stories. More than once he covered the World Series with rhymed stories sent out daily on the wire services. He was sent to France as a Special Correspondent for *Collier's* during World War I and in 1909 served briefly as an associate editor of *Puck*. In 1936 the Hearst papers ran a highly promoted ballad competition for music to two of his poems. He also edited a 10-volume anthology of *The World's 1000 Best Poems* (1929) for Funk & Wagnalls, and copyright records show that he even wrote lyrics for a Jerome Kern musical called "Toot-Toot"!

Although we have so far located and retrieved only a portion of Braley's work (much of the newspaper and magazine work may now be lost), more than enough is at hand now to judge him "outstanding" and to warrant this selected republication, lest Berton Braley's works be lost entirely. It is already very hard to find any of his work outside of rare book collections (save for three of his poems anthologized in the classic *Best Loved Poems of the American People*).

The immediate provocation for publishing this selected reissue was the response of audiences to my live dramatic performances of Braley's poetry—and my unwillingness to spend long hours in front of a copy machine after each performance, to satisfy the many requests for copies of the material. Posters of Braley's most popular poems have been produced recently by The Values Group, but still the requests for a book version have mounted.

Why have audiences responded so strongly, and why have we titled this small sampler of Braley's work "Virtues in Verse"? The answers to both questions involve reasons that operate on several levels.

On the level of poetic *craftsmanship*, Braley's virtuosity lies in his observance of the fundamentals of verse construction that it has become fashionable to omit in "modern" poetry: *everything* of Braley's *rhymes and scans*. With conscious intention he studied standards for the creation of well constructed verse, and he diligently worked to reflect those virtues in his own production. "When I had learned 'manner,' " he writes of his early self-tutoring, "I thought 'matter' would take care of itself. If I had the stuff, I was more likely to write poetry by first learning to write verse . . ."

Chiefly attracted by light verse, Braley wrote, "Half the fun of light verse *is* its pure virtuosity . . . I didn't think of myself as a poet, but as somebody who *might* become a versifier. I don't think of myself as a poet now (in which opinion many people concur) but—I did become a versifier. And a good one, if I do say it myself."

If you agree with this Editor that the best poetry is that which

- expresses an important thought, using
- vivid, memorable imagery, with
- verbal economy, and
- effectively exploits the "sound effects" of the language* (which in English come chiefly from rhyme and meter),

then you will have little quarrel with our dubbing Berton Braley "poet," who only called himself "versifier."

Another reason for the title of this volume is Braley's subject matter: explicitly or implicitly, much of his work celebrates the best in Man's nature and the achievements of which he is capable. The virtues of reason, honesty, independence, productivity, and pride shine out from the best of Braley's poems with a clarity—and a self-consciousness—found only rarely in modern literature (notably in the novels of Ayn Rand). They are the virtues and the values that engendered the Industrial Era—a time of vigor and vitality, of limitless vision creating boundless opportunities, of optimism founded on ability, of confidence built upon achievement. His poetry illustrates beautifully the unique power of fiction in the Romantic tradition to "paint a picture"—to inspire and instruct by *showing* heroic ideas *in action*—in contrast to non-fiction's mere lecturing.

A handful of Braley's poems dealing expressly with character traits are collected here under the "Virtues in Verse" subhead. Character traits also appear explicitly in a few of the poems praising particular "People & Places." But nearly all the poems in this book—from those celebrating the romance of productive achievement, arranged under "The Working World," to those showing the high "Adventure of Life," to his light-handed touch with romantic love sampled under

---

*a wonderful concept I first came across in a 1991 essay by John Enright.

"Lovers & Lasses"—at least implicitly project a *positive, inspiring vision of Man,* the *life that is possible to him,* and the *virtues of character* that are necessary to achieving that life.

Even the "Virtues Inverse" section, poems from Braley's 1936 book, *New Deal Ditties, or Running in the Red with Roosevelt,* demonstrates virtues by the potent device of ridiculing the vices of government interference. The topicality of *these* verses—in the Summer of 1993, with President Clinton's new "budget" and socialized medicine on the horizon—is almost *déjà vu.*

Indeed, after nearly a year of performing Braley's poetry live, I have grown increasingly impressed with the topicality of his messages. Never mind that some of the industrial technology he writes about may be obsolete; the *human nature* and *potential* that his verses reflect are universal and timeless. As he wrote in "Old Stuff":

> "For simple tests and practical bear out their truth didactical
> And as a working plan of life the copybooks are right!"

And a curious phenomenon, which I call "the Braley Effect," has emerged. It is principally manifested when those seized by it are heard to frequently interject into conversations, "Berton Braley has a poem about that . . ."

Most of the poems in this collection were selected from *Songs of the Workaday World* (1915), *Things As They Are* (1916), and *A Banjo at Armageddon* (1917)—all published by George H. Doran Co. (New York); *Hurdy Gurdy on Olympus,* D. Appleton & Co. (New York & London, 1927); and *New Deal Ditties, or Running in the Red with Roosevelt,* Greenberg (New York, 1936). The exceptions are the poems appearing on pages 5, 17, and 87 (all syndicated by N.E.A. in 1923) and those on page 11 (from the Stockton *Independent,* 1934), page 80 (*Green Book Magazine,* 1915), page 105 (Evansville, Indiana, *Press,* 1913), and page 160 (*Saturday Evening Post,* 1957). The poem on page 26 is from an old newsprint clipping in Braley's mother's scrapbook and appears to have been written before 1909. Braley's memoirs, *Pegasus Pulls a Hack: Memoirs of a Modern Minstrel,* was published in 1934 by Minton, Balch and Co. (New York).

My thanks to King Wiemann, who first posted three of Berton Braley's poems on the OSG computer bulletin board; to Anne Ladd, who picked those up and reprinted "The Thinker" in her *Cantique Connection,* where I first saw it, inspiring me to go looking for more;

and to all those audiences whose extraordinarily enthusiastic response to my performances of Braley's poetry sparked the production of this book. One of the most remarkable things about that response was the number of people who came forward and offered not only their encouragement, but their own time to help track down more of Braley's prolific writings. I am especially grateful to Stephen G. Floyd, a student in Austin, Texas, who became my principal research assistant and volunteered many days standing at a copy machine at the Library of Congress; without his enthusiastic efforts, this book could not have appeared so quickly. It was also King Wiemann, through his acquaintance with Linda Braley and her father-in-law (the "other" Berton Braley), who arranged for us to use the photograph of Gordon Stevenson's portrait of the poet (circa 1932) which appears on page xiv and the back cover. To Ian Braley, the poet's son, I am indebted for permission to use the pictures of his father that appear on pages iv and 110, as well as for allowing access to and copying of family scrapbooks, correspondence, and other materials. My thanks also to Frank Andorka, legal counsel for N.E.A., for his courteous cooperation in my research.

A special word of gratitude to my publisher, Patricia LeChevalier, of The Atlantean Press, for her dedication to bringing good literature in the Romantic tradition into print. Her vision is such that—on our first meeting, and after scanning no more than a dozen of Braley's poems—she readily agreed that we did, indeed, "have business to discuss"! And to Steve Klopfstein, who took the vision inside our heads of "Braley's World" and brought it to life with his wonderful cover illustration.

Editor's Dedication

For my father, Monte M. Abrams (1903-1966),
who first showed me the power of words, the
love of poetry, and the importance of reason.

Linda Tania Abrams
Los Angeles, September 1993

Berton Braley circa 1932, by Gordon Stevenson

THE THINKER

Back of the beating hammer
  By which the steel is wrought,
Back of the workshop's clamor
  The seeker may find the Thought,
The Thought that is ever master
  Of iron and steam and steel,
That rises above disaster
  And tramples it under heel!

The drudge may fret and tinker
  Or labor with lusty blows,
But back of him stands the Thinker,
  The clear-eyed man who knows;
For into each plow or saber,
  Each piece and part and whole,
Must go the Brains of Labor,
  Which gives the work a soul!

Back of the motors humming,
  Back of the belts that sing,
Back of the hammers drumming,
  Back of the cranes that swing,
There is the eye which scans them
  Watching through stress and strain,
There is the Mind which plans them—
  Back of the brawn, the Brain!

Might of the roaring boiler,
  Force of the engine's thrust,
Strength of the sweating toiler—
  Greatly in these we trust.
But back of them stands the Schemer,
  The Thinker who drives things through;
Back of the Job—the Dreamer
  Who's making the dream come true!

GRATITUDE

They sent me out in the wilderness to build 'em a
    power plant,
Where there wasn't a rail in thirty miles and the trails
    were rough and scant;
They sent me out with a trapper's map, and a husky,
    healthy gang,
That lived and worked from day to day and let all else
    go hang.
There wasn't a sign of a wagon road and the trail was
    a rocky track,
And we had to take machines apart in pieces a mule
    could pack.
So, slow and careful, we hiked along—and gee, what
    a weary tramp,
Till we reached the place I had planned the dam, and
    there we made our camp.

      The sad coyotes howled
        Like some uncanny choir,
      And bear and wildcat prowled
        Beyond our sleeping fire,
      But we—in slumber deep,
        We lay the whole night through,
      For men must get their sleep,
        When they have work to do.

The ice came down with the winter, the floods came
    down with the spring,
And we fought with that raging river as you fight with
    a living thing.
And we heckled the fat directors, back there in the
    busy town,
For they kept trying to stir us up, while keeping
    expenses down.

Whatever supplies we needed, of lumber, cement, or
 steel,
I had to beg and pray for in many a wild appeal.
And while we were bucking nature, in tempest and
 cold and heat,
The fat directors wired me, "Why isn't the job
 complete?"

> They'd fume and fuss and fret,
> And scold and interfere,
> While we—we simply sweat,
> And tried to keep our cheer.
> In spite of doubt, delay,
> And fat directors, too,
> We went right on our way,
> For we had work to do.

They sent me out in the wilderness to build 'em a
 power plant,
And it's running now as it ought to be, though some
 folks said "It can't!"
And now that everything's smooth and fine, they've
 fastened a can to me,
And they've put in a brand-new graduate, with a
 nice, fresh, school degree.
But say, it was fun while the job was on—a regular
 man's size game!—
For we built the dam and power plant, in spite of the
 bumps that came;
So the boy is welcome to have the job, and sit in the
 office chair—
There's a power plant in the wilderness, and I—I put
 it there!

THE POWER PLANT

Whirr! Whirr! Whirr! Whirr!
The mighty dynamos hum and purr,
And the blue flames crackle and glow and burn
Where the brushes touch and the magnets turn.
Whirr! Whirr! Whirr! Whirr!
This is no shrine of the Things That Were,
But the tingling altar of live To-day,
Where the modern priests of the "Juice" hold sway;
Where the lights are born and the lightnings made
To serve the needs of the world of trade.

Whirr! Whirr! Whirr! Whirr!
The white lights banish the murky blurr,
And over the city, far and near,
The spell extends that was conjured here,
While down in the wheel-pits, far below,
The water whirls in a ceaseless flow—
Foaming and boiling, wild and white,
In a passionate race of tireless might,
Rushing ever the turbines through,
And making the dream, the Dream come true!

Whirr! Whirr! Whirr! Whirr!
The dynamos croon and hum and purr,
And over the city's myriad ways
The jeweled lights all burst ablaze,
And the peak-load comes on the burdened wires
As the folk rush home to their food and fires!

Whirr! Whirr! Whirr! Whirr!
This is the heart of the city's stir,
Here where the dynamos croon and sing,
Here where only the "Juice" is King,
Where the switchboard stands in its marble pride,
And the tender watches it, argus-eyed;

Where Death is harnessed and made to serve
By keen-faced masters of brain and nerve;
This is the shrine of the God That Works,
Driving away the mists and murks,
Turning the lightnings into use.
This is the shrine of the mighty "Juice,"
Flowing ever the long wires through,
And making the dream, the Dream come true!

THE SHOPS

Factories are crude and ugly places
   Even at best, and most of them are filled,
With belts and shafts, machinery that races,
And men with heavy hands and grimy faces,
   And noise, noise, noise!—noise that is ever spilled
Upon the air like molten, white hot steel
   So fierce it is; noise that is ground and shrilled,
     Pounded and shrieked and hummed,
     Clattered and drummed—
Noise of the furnace and the hammer, squeal
   Of monster planers, crunch of giant shears,
   Rumble of rollers thudding on the ears
With most intolerable clamor, yet these places
Are where the dreams are built.
           —Through far flung spaces
The long trains thunder; over vasty seas
   The ships move on superbly; towers rise
   Graceful and strong against the arching skies
Of roaring cities,—miracles like these
   —All the huge wonders of this plangent time—
   Are born of ugly shops bedimmed with grime.

MAN

Weak and puny, small and frail,
Helpless he with tooth or nail,
In a world of fang and claw
Where sheer power makes the law.
Into battle he has gone
With the shaggy mastodon,
With the cruel beasts of prey
Snarling in their lust to slay,
Thirsting for the taste of blood;
He has fought with fire and flood,
With a heart and soul elate
Warred with nature—and with fate,
Dauntless, fearless, bold of eye,
Unafraid to fall and die,
Man has battled countless odds
Which would fright the very gods,
But by virtue of his will
Which no chill defeat could kill,
And by strength of heart and soul
He has striven to his goal;
By sheer vigor of attack
Beaten brute creation back
And through countless conflicts hurled
Made him Master of the World!

WHY NOT?

(With apologies to William Knox)

Why shouldn't the soul of a mortal be proud?
Life goes, it is true, like a swift-flying cloud
But while it is going and ere he has died
A man may do many things worthy of pride.

The high and the humble, the meek and the brave,
Are all of them destined, in time, to the grave,
But while they are living and drawing their breath
They may create something that lives after death.

The Builder may build and the Singer may sing,
The Painter may paint while his time's on the wing.
And when they are buried deep down in the grime
The things they have made will remain for all time.

Man conquers the mountains, the seas and the air,
And deserts turn gardens while under his care.
He does wondrous deeds in the scant space allowed;
Why shouldn't the soul of a mortal be proud?

Up out of the darkness we reach to the light
And slowly through ages we toil to the height.
The soul of a mortal is more than his clay;
The spirit of man can defy all decay!

So lift up your eyes to the Truth that is God's:
In spite of disaster, in face of all odds,
The spirit of Man is not wrapped in the shroud,
Why shouldn't the soul of a mortal be proud?

ENCHANTED MACHINES

The Slave of the Lamp that Aladdin once treasured
    Wrought wonders of magical skill,
Yet all of his marvels to-day are outmeasured
    By jinn who are mightier still.
Our jinn are the slaves of a switch or a lever,
    Who serve amid workaday scenes,
Who steadily, tirelessly, toil on forever—
    Uncanny, Enchanted Machines.

They fashion our needles, they spin our steel cables,
    They roll the great girders and rails;
They turn, build, and polish our chairs and our tables;
    They stamp out our kettles and pails.
They banish the dark at the touch of a finger,
    They bake us our bread and our beans;
They never rebel and they never malinger,
    Our slaves—the Enchanted Machines.

They spin, weave, and finish the clothes we are clad in;
    They multiply, add, and subtract;
They make every dream of the fabled Aladdin
    A tangible, commonplace fact.
The plowing is done and the broad fields are planted
    By laborers builded of steel,
Who work with a strength and a cunning enchanted
    No Slave of the Lamp could reveal!

Enchanted, in fact, with the only true magic—
    The magic that lives in the Brain,
By which man has banished his drudgery tragic,
    The sweat and the toil and the strain.
The magic that, seeking new visions, new courses,
    Knows not what "Impossible" means,
The magic that harnesses infinite forces
    And builds these Enchanted Machines!

THE TELEPHONE DIRECTORY

What is there seeming duller than this book,
　This stolid volume of prosaic print?
And yet it is a glass through which we look
　On wonderland and marvels without stint.
It is a key which will unlock the gate
　Of distance and of time and circumstance,
A wand that makes the wires articulate
　With hum of trade and whisper of romance!

Somehow there is enchantment in each page—
　The whirr of wheels, the murmurs of the mart,
The myriad mighty voices of the age,
　The throbbing of the great world's restless heart,—
Such are the sounds this volume seems to store
　For him who feels the magic of its thrall,
Who views the vistas it unrolls before
　His eyes that scarce can comprehend them all!

Here is the guide to all the vast extent
　The wires have bound together, this will show
The way to help when need is imminent,
　When terror threatens or when life burns low;
This brings the lover to his heart's desire,
　That he may speak to her o'er hill and lea,
This is the secret of the singing wire,
　To all the "world without" this is the key!

BUSINESS IS BUSINESS

"Business is Business," the Little Man said,
    "A battle where 'everything goes,'
Where the only gospel is 'get ahead,'
    And never spare friends or foes,
'Slay or be slain,' is the slogan cold,
    You must struggle and slash and tear,
For Business is Business, a fight for gold,
    Where all that you do is fair!"

"Business is Business," the Big Man said,
    "A battle to make of earth
A place to yield us more wine and bread
    More pleasure and joy and mirth;
There are still some bandits and buccaneers
    Who are jungle-bred beasts of trade,
But their number dwindles with passing years
    And dead is the code they made!

"Business is Business," the Big Man said,
    "But it's something that's more, far more;
For it makes sweet gardens of deserts dead,
    And cities it built now roar
Where once the deer and the grey wolf ran
    From the pioneer's swift advance;
Business is Magic that toils for man
    Business is True Romance.

"And those who make it a ruthless fight
    Have only themselves to blame
If they feel no whit of the keen delight
    In playing the Bigger Game,
The game that calls on the heart and head,
    The best of man's strength and nerve;
Business is Business," the Big Man said,
    "And that Business is to serve!"

REPORTER'S ENVOI

Column in the *Stockton Independent*, October 27, 1934:

The Observer by E. E. L.

Because the boss has a place for real poetry on his own page, the Observer generally shies away from it, but he just was shown some verses that he likes a lot, because they tell more about the newspaper reporters than 50 million movies or 20,000 criticisms.

Written by Berton Braley, the verses are a take-off on Kipling's famous 'L'Envoi,' and say what most reporters would say if they could say it as well. It's called the 'Reporter's Envoi.':

When earth's last paper is printed and the forms and the metals
    are cold,
When the newest scandal is ancient, and the last extra is sold,
We shall loaf—and Lord, how we need it! With nothing at all
    to do,
Till the Boss of the perfect paper shall call us to work anew.

And then we shall work as we'd like to, each on his own machine.
And the truth shall be in our copy, and nothing shall intervene.
We shall write real stories about them—beggar and millionaire—
For an Editor keen and fearless, a paper that's on the square.

We shall work in a rush and hurry, for that is the Goodly Game,
And we shall not dig in the gutter for stories of filth and shame;
And the copy readers above us shall leave our "features" alone,
And the stories that fill the columns we shall recognize as our own!

We shall have no fool assignments, no cruel missions of pain,
To torture the broken-hearted, or blacken the sinner's stain;
We shall scoop and be scooped aplenty; we shall love the flurry
    and noise,
We shall fight with the business office and fuss with the copy boys;
But each of us shall be human, and each of us shall be free
To write the thing as he sees it for the Paper That Ought To Be.

THE WORKING SONG

(After Chesterton)

Oh, we're sick to death of the style of song
   That's only a sort of a simpering song,
A kissy song and a sissy song
   Or a weepy, creepy, whimpering song.
So give us the lift of a lusty song,
   A boisterous, bubbling, boiling song,
Or a smashing song and a dashing song,
   Oh, give us the tang of a toiling song,
The chanty loud of the working crowd,
   The thunderous thrall of a toiling song!

Ay, sing us a joyous daring song,
   Not a moaning, groaning, fretting song,
But a ringing song, and a swinging song,
   A rigorous, vigorous, sweating song.
We have had enough of the gypsy song,
   Which is only a lazy, shirking song,
So toughen your throat to a rougher note
   And give us the tune of a working song,
A tune of strife and the joy of life,
   The beat and throb of a working song!

MERCENARIES

They come from all over the planet,
   An Army that's never at rest,
Wherever a job is, they man it,
   In East, North or South or the West.
The Wops and the Slavs and the Limeys
   The Hunkies and Micks and the Yanks,
Where dust, sweat and labor and grime is
   They battle in militant ranks.

They war with the desert and river,
   They fight with the quag and the rock,
Their blows make a continent shiver,
   And mountains are split by the shock;
They lift the steel over the ridges,
   They dam up the floods coming down,
They fling forth the trestles and bridges,
   They burrow 'neath torrent and town.

Big-chested, big-hearted, big-handed,
   They march to the furthest frontiers
And there they perform as commanded
   Without any salvoes of cheers.
A hard-thewed and rough aggregation
   A mixed and a polyglot mob
Who battle for civilization
   —This Army of Men on the Job!

READY!

Here we are, gentlemen; here's the whole gang of us,
    Pretty near through with the job we are on;
Size up our work—it will give you the hang of us—
    South to Balboa and north to Colon.
Yes, the canal is our letter of reference;
    Look at Culebra and glance at Gatun;
What can we do for you—got any preference,
    Wireless to Saturn or bridge to the moon?

Don't send us back to a life that is flat again,
    We who have shattered a continent's spine;
Office work—Lord, but we couldn't do that again!
    Haven't you something that's more in our line?
Got any river they say isn't crossable?
    Got any mountains that can't be cut through?
We specialize in the wholly impossible,
    Doing things "nobody ever could do!"

Take a good look at the whole husky crew of us,
    Engineers, doctors and steam-shovel men;
Taken together you'll find quite a few of us
    Soon to be ready for trouble again.
Bronzed by the tropical sun that is blistery,
    Chockful of energy, vigor and tang,
Trained by a task that's the biggest in history,
    Who has a job for this Panama gang?

U. S. RECLAMATION ENGINEERS

—Phoenix, Arizona

Here, where once a desert lay, desolate and bare,
Now a glad green country smiles, opulent and fair;
Floods that thundered madly down, raging through the land,
Now are held and leashed by Man, serving his command.
    So a miracle appears,
      Where the cactus ruled for half-a-million years,
        Over dusty trails forlorn,
        Now there's cotton, wheat and corn,
    Thanks to U. S. Reclamation Engineers!

Here where lean coyotes howled, where mesquite had spread
Over league on barren league, thirsty, bleak and dead,
There are farms and villages, churches, homes and schools,
All because the engineers learned to use their tools.
    So a miracle—a miracle appears.
      And the driest land upon the hemispheres
        Comes to blossom as the rose,
        Growing everything that grows,
    Thanks to U. S. Reclamation Engineers!

Manna in the wilderness, water on the plain,
That's what engineers have brought to this broad domain.
Dam and ditch and deep canal where the waters run,
They have wrought their magic under Arizona's sun.
    So a miracle—a miracle appears,
      And the desert wind that withers up and sears,
        Has become a gentle breeze,
        Sighing gently through the trees,
    Thanks to U. S. Reclamation Engineers!

LEATHER LEGGIN'S

Whin you want to build a railroad through the jungle or the veldt
   Where there's niver anybody bin before,
Why you call on Leather Leggin's, an' he hitches up his belt
   An' he takes it as his ordinary chore
To go slashin' through the forests, where the monkeys chatter shrill,
   An' the lazy snakes are hissin' down below,
Or to drag a chain an' transit over gulch and grassy hill,
   As he marks the route the right-av-way will go!

He's a nervy, wiry divil, with his notebook an' his livil,
   An' he doesn't seem to know the name av fear,
He's a sort av scout av Progress, on the payroll as a civil—
   (Though he ain't so awful civil, if you say it on the livil!)
     On the payroll as a Civil Engineer!

Whin you need to dam a river, or to turn it upside down,
   Or to tunnel underneath it in the mud,
Or to bore an' blast a subway through the innards av a town,
   Or to blow aside a mountain with a thud;
When you want to bridge a canyon where there ain't no place
     to cling,
   An' the cliffs is steep an' smoother than a wall,
Why, you call on Leather Leggin's, an' he does that little thing,
   An' then comes around an' asks you, "Is that all?"

Oh, he always has a fire in his old an' blackened briar,
   An' he tackles anny job that may appear,
An' he does it on the livil, this here divil of a Civil—
   (Though he ain't so very civil, if you put it on the livil!)
     This here divil av a Civil Engineer!

Now the bankers down in Wall Street gits the profits whin it's done,
   While us heavy-futted diggers gits the can,
But we lifts our hats respectful to the Ingineer, my son,
   For that feller, Leather Leggin's, is a Man!

Yes, he takes a heap o' chances, and he works like Billy Hell,
  An' his job is neither peaceable nor tame,
But you bet he knows his business an' he does it mighty well,
  An' I want to give him credit for the same!

He is plucky—on the livil—and you'll niver hear him snivel,
  Though Fate does her best to put him in the clear,
He's the Grit that niver flinches—on the payroll as a Civil,
(For he's sometimes pretty civil, an' he's always on the livil!)
  On the payroll as a Civil Engineer!

BLUEPRINTS

These are the charts of dreams that shall come true,
  These are the plans from which there shall arise
Towers that lift their heads against the skies,
  Ships for wide seas, and planes to ride the blue.
Floods shall obey, tunnels be driven through
  Eternal rock, the wilderness that lies
Unpeopled, shall awake to high emprise,
  And all the world shall be made over new.

Under the magic guidance of these charts,
  Marking in lines and figures what the brain
Of man conceived. They are a mystic key
  To unimagined riches, lovelier arts,
To hopes we seek and goals we shall attain,
  These blueprint epics of the days to be!

THE STEEL-WORKER

Wherever new bridges are flinging
    Their spider-web skein to the skies;
Where the steel ships are made for the business of trade;
    Where the skyscrapers gauntly arise;
Where the cranes lift the twenty-ton girders
    And the red rivets hiss through the air—
From Chile to Nome and from China to Rome,
    The steel-worker's sure to be there.

      "Hey you!"
        (So the foreman said)
      "Watch the way you're doin' there;
        Use your bloomin' head.
      Lower her! Now—let 'er go!
        Ram the rivets through."
      (That's the way they do the job,
        Do it proper, too.)

This week you will find him on Broadway
    Some forty floors upward or so,
Where the men seem to crawl on just nothing at all
    When you watch from the sidewalk below.
Next week he'll be starting for Egypt,
    This viewer of cities and men,
With his money all spent he is fully content
    So long as he's moving again.

      "Hey you!"
        (Hear the foreman call)
      "Swing her over—hold her there!
        Hoist a bit—that's all.
      Drop her now, but drop her slow.
        Now you've got her true."
      (That's the way they do the job,
        Do it proper, too.)

His passport's the card of his union
　　Wherever he happens to land,
His home is the spot where a job's to be got,
　　For the skill of his head and his hand;
No task is too distant to tackle,
　　No chance too outlandish or dim;
He carelessly goes like the wind as she blows,
　　And the world has no terrors for him.

　　　　"Hey you!"
　　　　　　(Hear the foreman shout)
　　　　"Watch that girder overhead!
　　　　　　Clear the Way—LOOK OUT!
　　　　Hi, you fool, get out o' that!
　　　　　　Almost got him—whew!"
　　　　(That's the way they do the job,
　　　　　　Do it proper, too.)

. . . *He is no sentimental observer of the working world, but a bona fide member of it; he sings of miners, steel workers, sailors, cowpunchers, reporters and tramps—and the songs ring true.*

New York *Tribune*, March 25, 1918

THE SONG OF THE AERONAUT

Up from the emerald turf I rise to the lure of the
    arching blue,
With a song in my heart like the ancient song the
    great Olympians knew.
While I steady myself on wings of white to the rush
    of the roving breeze,
Tempting the wrath of the infinite, the marvelous
    weightless seas;
Below me the world is a blur of green, a flicker of
    brown and red,
And the vault of the sky is mine to try and the
    limitless vast ahead!
It's sport that only the birds have known who poise
    in the upper day,
But now I challenge their airy throne—these kings
    of the blue highway!

I buffet my route through winds that shout, I dip to
    the billows of air,
And mock me the hawk and the pirate bird that
    hover in wonder there.
Disdainful I sweep above mortals who creep like
    worms on the overturned clod,
And serenely I soar in the empire of space—an
    insolent, strong-winged god!
The purr of the motors, the shiver of wires and the
    lift of the quivering planes,
As I clamber the sides of aerial hills and swoop
    down aerial lanes,
Stir all my blood to a turbulent flood till all that is
    earthly of me
Is lost in a rapture of speed and of flight—I am free,
    I am free, I am free!

For mine is no road that is meted and bound, but the
way of the wind and the sky,
Beyond all the dust and the fret and the heat, above
all the clamor I fly
To the height where the hawk circles wary and lone,
to the vault where the bald eagles scream,
Where the fetters of earth and the worries of earth
are dim in the haze of a dream.
Then sudden I drop toward the world I have left and
the wind whistles keen through the frame,
Or I wheel and I swing in a glorious ring on a trail
that is never the same.
Oh, danger is mine in this frolic divine as I dare all
the forces that slay,
But mine is the song of the free and the strong—the
Lord of the Blue Highway!

THE ELECTRICIAN

Where the sparks of the white-hot welder play,
Where the searchlights stab at the fogbank grey,
Where the bright lights glare on the Great White Way,
    The Slave of the Lamp is lurking,
The Slave of the Lamp, yet the Master too,
The wizard of light in a world made new
Where the fairy tales of the past come true
    And the dreams of the past are working!

The power house is his charge to keep,
Where the dynamos whir and the blue sparks leap,
And death is waiting—if caution sleep—
    In the midst of the day's endeavour,
For if ever that harnessed might breaks loose
From the chains that hold it bound for use,
The Slave of the Lamp—and Boss of the Juice—
    Is done with the Job, forever!

He tinkers away at the trolley wire
Or jauntily dares the third rail's ire,
That things may run to his heart's desire
    And the work of the world hold steady.
Would you hire a man who is schooled to jolts,
Who can play ping pong with the thunderbolts
And juggle away with a million volts?
    The Slave of the Lamp is ready!

THE FARMER

When all the songs of labor have been sung
   (Full of the clang of steel, the throb of steam,
The clatter of the hammers where is flung
   The fine spun bridge across the roaring stream)
When all the chants of labor have been said
   (Deep throated chants from mighty bosoms hurled)
Mine is the chant of chants, the Song of Bread
   I am the Master—for I feed the World!

The toilers of the factories and mines
   The workers of the rivers and the seas,
The heavy-muscled hewers of the pines,
   The idlers 'mid their unearned luxuries,
At last must look to Me, aye, one and all
   Without me armies fail and flags are furled,
Without me kingdoms die and Empires fall,
   I am the Master, for I feed the World!

Beneath the blazing sun I do my toil
   With straining back and overburdened thews,
Sowing the seed and reaping from the soil
   The corn and wheat and rice that men must use,
Patient and strong I bend me to my work,
   Life eddies round me like a dust-cloud whirled,
For this I know, despite the sweat and irk,
   I am the Master, for I feed the World!

AT A WAR HOSPITAL

Doctor, here's a man without a jaw;
    Doctor, here's a chap without a cheek,
Battered up by shrapnel, bleeding raw,
    Smelling of the battle's smoke and reek;
Doctor, here's a leg that's torn to scraps;
    Here's a hand that's hanging by a thread.
What's the final verdict on these chaps
    Waiting while their bandages grow red?

Well, they're not pleasant to look at—covered with
    vermin and mud,
Battered and mangled and shattered, scarlet or
    blackened with blood;
Still it's our business to mend them, build them all
    over again,
Forming these terrible fragments back into brothers
    and men;
Framing a jawbone of rubber, growing a cheek from a
    scar;
Routing the germs of infection, fighting the horrors
    of war,
All of our training and science meeting the instant
    demand,
Wasting no moments in pity—pity unsteadies the
    hand—
Calm and unfeeling and certain, knowing the things
    we must do.
Such is the work of the surgeon—making men over
    anew!

Here's a chap that's torn from head to heels;
    Death has got him hanging on the brink,
Yet he always answers that he feels
    Simply "In the pink, sir, in the pink!"
Grinning if they have a mouth to grin,
    Winking very gaily if it's gone;
That's the kind of men they're bringing in;
    That's the type of lad we're working on.

Yet we must take them as "cases"—work that is here
    to be done,
Each as a sort of a battle—struggle that has to be won,
Smashed by the scattering shrapnel, hand grenades,
    bullets and shells,
Victims of gunfire and gases worse than a number of
    hells;
These are the fellows we tackle, taking what fragments
    there be,
Forming them back into humans fit for their sweethearts
    to see,
Splicing their nerves and their muscles, rebuilding
    tissue and bone,
Making strange surgical magic hitherto almost
    unknown;
There is a joy in our labors, though they are grisly
    to do;
We are the miracle workers—making men over anew!

THE SONG OF THE LOCOMOTIVE

The furnace roared and clamored when the frame of me was cast,
    The hammers trampled ingots under heel,
The clanging rollers rumbled as they clutched the bars that passed,
    'Till I stood a panting giant, wrought of steel.
Then the engineer, my master, clambered to his leather seat
    And slowly through the busy yards I drew,
'Till the mail train was complete and I felt my air-pump beat,
    As they coupled me and bade me "Take-'er-through."

    "Clear block! Clear block!" the signals glare
        "Side track all trains and let me by."
    And over switch and bridge I tear
        My headlight like a cyclop's eye—
    I am the king of the gleaming rail
    For I pull the cars of the Overland Mail.

When I leave the smoky city I must hold my strength in check
    Where the interlocking switches clank and jar;
But when I strike the open, oh it's then for me to "trek"
    As the sweating mail clerks labor in the car.
Then the flanges hold me faithful to the track that men have laid
    And my whistle shrieks a warning far and near,
And my frame is rocked and swayed as I shoot o'er flat and glade
    At the bidding of my lord, the Engineer!

    "Clear block! Clear block!" the signals say;
        The Limited itself must wait
    To let me have my sovereign way
        And go my mile-a-minute gait!
    I am the one who makes the trail
    For the long blind cars of the Overland Mail.

Over trestles, through the tunnels, past the villages asleep,
    With my grunting fireman stoking me like mad,
I'm a happy giant singing as across the miles I sweep
    For the strength and speed within me make me glad!
So the train dispatcher routes me, "Sidetrack all for Number 1!"
    And the lantern-swinging switchman does his best,
'Till my flaring race is done as I end the nightly run
    And I amble to the roundhouse for a rest.

        "Clear block! Clear block!" the signals glow,
            The right of way is mine! is mine!
        Expresses swift and locals slow
            Must wait me all along the line.
        I am the one whom the watchers hail
        "Ah, there he goes with the Overland Mail!"

TO A PHOTOGRAPHER

I have known love and hate and work and fight;
    I have lived largely, I have dreamed and planned,
    And Time, the Sculptor, with a master hand
Has graven on my face for all men's sight
Deep lines of joy and sorrow, growth and blight
    Of labor and of service and command
    —And now you show me this, this waxen, bland
And placid face, unlined, unwrinkled, white.

This is not I—this fatuous thing you show,
    Retouched and smoothed and prettified to please,
Put back the wrinkles and the lines I know;
    I have spent blood and tears achieving these,
Out of the pain, the struggle and the wrack
These are my scars of battle—put them back!

BALLADE OF THE IDEAL WAITER

Some people sigh for a waiter who's humble,
  Fawning and cringing and honied and sweet,
One who will smirk though you sputter and grumble
  Kicking at everything offered to eat;
  Others like garçons most proud and élite
Waiters who radiate hauteur and tone,
  Some people ask for a servant who's fleet,
I want a waiter who'll let me alone.

I want a waiter who'll forbear to fumble
  Glasses and spoons as I loll in my seat,
One who won't lean over closely and mumble
  Hints of things needed my meal to complete;
  One who will stay at a distance discreet,
Not stick as close as a dog to a bone,
  One who won't walk up and down—and repeat!—
I want a waiter who'll let me alone!

Yea, he may spot me with soup, he may stumble
  Spilling my viands and treading my feet,
His voice may be only an insolent rumble,
  His fingernails black and his checking a cheat,
  But oh, if he'll leave me in peace at my meat,
Till I'm ready to go—and have made the fact known,
  A generous tip shall be his for the treat,
I want a waiter who'll let me alone!

ENVOY

Prince, let's get off of our usual beat,
  Let us find out if my vision has flown.
There's a small cafeteria just down the street
  —I want a waiter who'll leave me alone.

THE POETESS

Oh smother me under your kisses,
    Your kisses that crackle and burn
With fervor so hot that it hisses,
    Demanding a sizzling return,
Oh, seize me and clasp me and take me
    With merciless force to your breast
And crush me so tight that you break me
    With strength that is brutal—but blest.

Oh, love me with pulsating passion,
    Regardless of life and of death.
And clutch me in feverish fashion
    So close that I falter for breath.
Your flaming eyes hold and enslave me.
    I writhe in your arms and I swoon
And the tides of forgetfulness lave me
    In the sheen of the palpitant moon.

My hair is a net to ensnare you,
    My arms are a withe to enfold,
My lips are a—"Sir! Why, how *dare* you!
    What reason have you to be bold!
My verses, you say, are so shady,
    Erotic and fiery?—Maybe,
But as for *myself*, I'M a lady
    So don't get familiar with me."

A PANTOUM OF REHEARSAL

Ladies, we'll try that again.
  Sing, for the Love of Mike, sing!
Hi there, you bum chorus men,
  You've got to *work* in this thing.

Sing, for the Love of Mike, sing!
  Quit falling over your feet.
You've got to *work* in this thing;
  One—two—three—four—and repeat.

Quit falling over your feet—
  Say, could you dance on a bet?
One—two—three—four and repeat
  —Now for the little soubrette.

Say, could you dance on a bet?
  Let's have the milliner's song;
Now comes the little soubrette—
  No, no, you're singing it wrong!

Let's have the milliner's song.
  Wow! But you're rotten to-day!
No, no—you're singing it wrong;
  It won't get over that way!

Wow! but you're rotten to-day—
  Worse than you commonly are.
It won't get over that way—
  Where in the hell is the star?

(Worse than you commonly are)
  Gee, but you give me a pain!
Where in the hell is the star?
  Oh, how de do, Miss Elaine!

(Gee, but you give me a pain;
    Making the crowd of us wait)
Oh, how de do, Miss Elaine!
    Oh no, you're not very late.

(Making the crowd of us wait—
    This thing is growing a bore.)
Oh no, you're not very late,
    Now, let's get busy once more!

This thing is growing a bore.
    Hi there, you bum chorus men!
Now let's get busy once more—
    Ladies, we'll try that again!

"Toot-Toot!" . . . deserves long life in the kingdom
of musical comedy . . .

    The show . . . bore evidence of long and faithful
rehearsals . . . Berton Braley's lyrics show his usual
grasp of the whims of the hour . . .

Evening Sun, March, 1918

THE POINT OF VIEW

He had toiled in the furnace glare
    Where the white hot metal glows,
He had done a grader's share
    In the road camp's dust and snows,
He had known the deep mines' murk
    And the threat of the lurking damp.
He had sweated at sailors' work
    On the decks of a deep-sea tramp.

So, having some gift of song,
    He sang of these chaps he knew,
A chant of the toiling throng
    With the world's rough jobs to do,
And the critics said, "Ah yes,
    Here's a note that is loud enough
To curry some cheap success
    With people who like such stuff.

"As jingles they're fairly wrought,
    But they do not smack of the soil,
For this troubadour hasn't caught
    The spirit and soul of toil."
And the singer read—and grinned
    And the workers, fagged and spent,
Sweating and grimy skinned,
    Knew not what the critics meant.
But the singer's songs they knew,
    And it was to *them* he sang;
And if *they* found them true—
    To hell with the critic gang!

THE SINGER'S DEFIANCE

Life, you have harried and hurt and scourged me,
   Mocked me cruelly through the years.
Under a burden of woe submerged me,
   Sought to fright me with pain and tears,
Fortune and glory you have denied me,
   Love you gave me—and took away,
Yet, for all of the years you've tried me,
   Dauntless I sing to the world today.

For out of the wreck of a vanished passion,
   Out of the failure, the doubt, the pain,
Out of the sorrow and death I'll fashion
   Many a song in a fearless strain,
And the songs I make shall have no savor
   Of useless longing or vain regret,
But I shall carol to make men braver
   For every trial that must be met.

Failure, defeat, despair—I know them,
   But still I challenge them, unafraid,
And men shall battle and overthrow them,
   Perchance because of a song I've made;
Life—though my peace and my joy be taken,
   Though all my visions and dreams go by,
I'll lift my voice in a tone unshaken
   And keep on singing until I die!

OPPORTUNITY

With doubt and dismay you are smitten
  You think there's no chance for you, son?
Why, the best books haven't been written
  The best race hasn't been run,
The best score hasn't been made yet,
  The best song hasn't been sung,
The best tune hasn't been played yet,
  Cheer up, for the world is young!

No chance? Why the world is just eager
  For things that you ought to create.
Its store of true wealth is still meagre
  Its needs are incessant and great,
It yearns for more power and beauty
  More laughter and love and romance,
More loyalty, labor and duty,
  No chance—why there's nothing but chance!

For the best verse hasn't been rhymed yet,
  The best house hasn't been planned,
The highest peak hasn't been climbed yet,
  The mightiest rivers aren't spanned,
Don't worry and fret, faint hearted,
  The chances have just begun,
For the Best jobs haven't been started,
  The Best work hasn't been done.

THE PIONEERS

They're the "utterly foolish dreamers,"
    Who dream of a better day;
They're not the plotters and schemers
    Who work for glory and pay,
But with confidence undiminished
    They dream of a world made new,
And after their days are finished
    The wonderful dream comes true!

They're the fighters who fight undaunted
    For the utterly hopeless cause,
Ridiculed, jeered and taunted,
    With never a lull or pause;
But after they've fought and perished,
    And after their work is done,
The cause they have loved and cherished
    Is lifted to fame—and won!

They know the hope and the yearning,
    The sting of the blind world's scorn,
But never the sunshine burning,
    The skies of their visioned morn;
They're the warriors fine and splendid,
    The fond and the faithful few,
Whose battles and work are ended,
    Or ever the dreams come true!

OUR LADY OF CHANGE

Sometimes she's a merry young hoyden,
    A madcap—fair brimming with fun—
Till sudden she shifts in her fancy and lifts
    The sober gray eyes of a Nun;
Her moods are as wayward as winds are,
    They change like the leaping of flame,
And for all of the grace of her form and her face,
    She's never exactly the same!

Sometimes she's a priestess and sibyl
    With eyes that are brooding and sad,
Or a gypsy girl fair with a rose in her hair,
    Or the laughing young Love of a lad,
Sometimes she's Our Lady of Sorrows
    Who's drunken of life to the lees,
Or a Will-o'-the-wisp just as light as the lisp
    Of the leaves of the whispering trees.

I've found her as true as a mother,
    I've known her as false as a jade,
As proud and serene as a panoplied queen,
    As simple and sweet as a maid—
So here's to My Lady Adventure
    Whose magic I may not defy,
By hill and by hollow her footsteps I follow,
    And so I shall do till I die!

THE GREAT ADVENTURE

(With acknowledgments to George Matthew Arnold)

What is the profit that men can find
    In the frozen North or the jungle heat?
What is the vision they hold in mind
    When they face the hardships that they must meet?
It cannot pay, yet they see it through
    And the magic purpose that keeps them to it,
Is doing the work that they want to do
    In the way that they want to do it.

It isn't money, it isn't fame,
    That stirs the soul to a true adventure,
Or makes men stick to the grimmest game
    In spite of ridicule, doubt and censure.
It's just the spirit that holds you true
    To what you've started, and bears you through it;
It's doing the work that you want to do
    In the way that you want to do it.

Oh, the weary souls who are chained by chance
    To a treadmill track they must always amble,
Who never thrilled to a mad romance,
    Who feared the risk of a mighty gamble.
They are the failures in life, not those
    Who dreamed and struggled and risked and lost,
Who toiled and battled and baked and froze
    But never flinched when the dice were tossed.

It's the thought that lifts us above the beast,
    The dream that moves us to discontent,
The thing that's driven us west and east
    And conquered ocean and continent;
And when we win to the heaven true
    We'll find a place, when we come to view it,
Where men do work that they want to do
    In the way that they want to do it!

MERCHANT ADVENTURERS

*(with acknowledgments to
Simeon Strunsky for the theme)*

Merchant Adventurers sending their galleys
    Seaward from Sidon and Tyre,
Freighting their wares over mountains and valleys,
    Desert and jungle and mire.
Merchant Adventurers—traders of Venice
    Peddling their goods overseas,
Dauntless in face of the terrors that menace;
    Merchant Adventurers, these!

Merchant Adventurers—"English Exploiters"
    Sailing the perilous Main,
Threading the haunts where the Buccaneer loiters,
    Dodging the galleons of Spain.
Merchant Adventurers—dealers and jobbers,
    German, Italian and Gaul,
Fighting the greedy baronial robbers
    —Merchant Adventurers, all!

Merchant Adventurers! All through the ages
    Somehow their business was done,
(Seeking their profit and paying their wages)
    Everywhere under the sun.
Jasons of trade who were ceaselessly faring
    Over new countries and seas,
Shopkeepers canny, courageous and daring,
    Merchant Adventurers, these!

Now? Writers damn them as "commonplace Babbitts,
    Clogging the path of advance,
Middle-class dullards of standardized habits,
    Utterly lacking romance!"
If we believe all these critics and censurers
    Business is humdrum to-day,
Gone is the spirit of Merchant Adventurers
    Crumbled to dust and decay!

Don't you believe it—that spirit is glowing
    Under the Business Man's vest;
Jasons of Trade are still joyously going
    Forth on a magical quest.
Gambling with Fate, burning bridges behind them,
    Wagering all in the till,
Bucking the world for a profit, you'll find them
    Merchant Adventurers still!

ADVENTURERS OF SCIENCE

With a microscope and a butterfly net and a specimen
    case they go
Into the heart of an African swamp or a jungle in
    Borneo.
Or with shovel and pick where the sand lies thick
    over cities a long time dead,
They dig down deep where the dead kings sleep—to
    learn of the lives they led.
They climb to the crest of Everest, they freeze in the
    arctic night,
To weigh the air of the mountain-peak, or see that a
    map reads right.
With tube and retort they grimly sport with poison or
    deadly germs
In order to write a monograph in highly technical
    terms.

        Spectacled "Profs" from colleges
           "Fusty and bookish-brained,"
        Probing wherever knowledge is
           Likely to be obtained.
        Sifting the old mythologies,
           Testing the dreams of youth,
        Experts in all the "ologies"
           Trudging the trail of Truth!

Their bones are strewn mid caverns hewn by the
    Paleolithic man,
They have died on the trail of the rumored vale
    where the Aryan race began;
Fever and drouth in the blistering South, the storms
    of the cruel North,
Have taken toll ere they reached their goal, but—
    their brethren still go forth!

They have suffered cancer to learn its cause, died
    lepers to seek a cure,
In quest of "basic natural laws" there's nothing they
    won't endure.
"Theorists, highbrows and logothetes" who
    nevertheless will dare
The ends of earth and the gates of death—if
    Knowledge is waiting there!

> Little of fame they get for it,
>   And poor they live—and die.
> Knowledge they seek—and sweat for it
>   That the world may gain thereby,
> The world that learns but tardily
>   And grudgingly too, in sooth;
> While ever these "pedants" hardily
>   Fare forth on the trail of Truth!

THE ADVENTURER

City of power and city of might,
Of plunder and passion and woe and delight,
The sound of your voice is a trumpeter's blare,
A challenge that's flung on the palpitant air,
A pæan of battle, a taunt, and a call
To join in the conflict and conquer—or fall.
To thrust and to parry, to feint and to lunge;
So—into the tumult I plunge!

I fear you?—the city of opulent dreams—
Because of your vastness that pulses and teems?
Why, here are my hands, they are young, they are strong
As any two hands in the thick of the throng;
And here are my eyes and my body and brain
Alert for the glory and gold I shall gain.
So—fearless I face you, O huge, roaring brute,
Besotted with splendor and glutted with loot!

What peril of jungle or desert or sea
Has more of a thrill than your dangers to me,
Or greater romance than the conflict that rolls
On your vast battlefield of a myriad souls?

I cry you defiance! Your masters and slaves,
Your wasters and delvers and dreamers and knaves,
I war for your palaces, pleasures and pelf;
I fear you no whit—for I fear not myself;
I face you and fight you, nor whimper for aid,
Since you crawl to the feet of the man unafraid!

THE WATCHERS

The trains go roaring past by day and flashing by at night
Bearing adventurers of trade or seekers of delight,
While from the little houses that front the right of way
There gaze the folks whom destiny has planted there to stay.
And some are wistful, wondering how it would seem to be
Click-clicking over shining rails, of every fetter free,
They thrill with dreaming vision of towns and fields afar
Which come to those who flicker past upon a Pullman car.

Yet most of those who watch the trains are scarcely stirred at all,
For them these magic chariots have neither spell nor thrall;
Their passage only serves to break the round of things and then
Dull-eyed the watchers go about their humdrum life again.
No longing leaps within their breasts, no envy fills their glance,
They never see in rushing trains the lure of high romance,
They only mutter, "she's on time" or "she's a little late,"
While great adventure thunders past their very dooryard gate!

Oh, sad it is for watchers who are wistful as they gaze
On many windowed caravans that sweep down metaled ways,
Yet though they never take that trail the dream is theirs to hold,
The thought to nurse and cherish and the vision to unfold,
But for the other watchers, the dull phlegmatic kind,
Theirs is the greater tragedy, for they are wholly blind,
And what could be so sad as they whose lives are bleak and slow
Who never know the world is wide—and do not want to know!

THE SAFETY VALVE

There's something in us, every one,
    A queer unrest that gets us all,
And till the game of life is done
    It irritates and frets us all.
Some seek to drown it deep in drink
    Despite the carpers' caviling;
And some in crime and some in—ink;
    I'm travelling, just travelling!

The gambler's joy is in the game,
    The lover's in his amorous
And fervid wooing. Some for fame
    And all it means are clamorous.
I leave the statesman to his state,
    The chairman to his gavelling,
The while with heart and mind elate
    I'm travelling, just travelling.

From land to land, from sea to sea
    Where life is brightest, breeziest,
I take the road that seems to me
    The kindest and the easiest;
And so, though swiftly, day by day
    My skein of life's unravelling,
I'll still be gayly on my way
    Travelling, just travelling!

---

*Forty-four hundred miles in 40 days in a flivver
was the remedy Berton Braley, the poet whose
works appear in* The Daily News, *took to cure his
restlessness.*

    Braley arrived in San Francisco today . . .
                 San Francisco *Daily News*

A SPECK ON THE DOT

Maybe this world is the tiniest dot
   In the limitless field of space
But at present it's all of the world I've got
   And a curious sort of place;
And though I've been over its realms a bit,
   There's plenty more left to see;
It may be a dot in the infinite
   But a sizable dot to me!

Yes, I'm only a speck on the dot, they say,
   But little enough I care,
I'm a speck that moves in its own sweet way
   On the trails that I choose to fare;
And as long as the world has sights to view
   Or mysteries left to know,
I'll do the things that a speck can do
   And go where a speck can go.

So this infinitesimal dot, the World,
   Seems wondrously big and strange
With the torrents of life about it swirled,
   And its dramas that shift and change;
It'll take me all of my years to trace
   The trails that are calling me.
And as for the trip through the rest of space
   I've got all eternity.

RED MEAT

These tales full of rancorous cankering
   Of peevishness, jaundice, and bile,
They give me a pain. I am hankering
   For stuff of more glamorous style.
Od's bodkins; S'Death! I'm fed up upon
   This food, realistic and stale,
I want some raw beefsteak to sup upon
   I want a fine swashbuckling tale,
         An "Up-clubs-and-bat-'em-all,
         Out-swords-and-at-'em-all"
            Tale.

Hi! buckoes, tremendous and swaggering
   With lace at your necks and your wrists,
Get busy with fencing and daggering;
   Come bravoes, reënter the lists.
Out, rapiers flashing and shimmering
   To fight for some popular frail
Whose eyes with enchantment are glimmering.
   Oh, give me a swashbuckling tale;
         A "Thrust-and-that's-done-for-you,
         Lady-I've-won-for-you"
            Tale.

Come, pirates of bloodiest memory,
   With all of your murderous pack
Whose hearts were much harder than emery,
   Whose oaths were much blacker than black.
Come on, do your stuff, be unbearable,
   "Git hung" at the end without fail,
I want to be thrilled something terrible;
   I long for a swashbuckling tale;
         An "Oh-boy, the-throes-of-it,"
         Clinch-at-the-close-of-it
            Tale.

THE JOY OF LIFE

I'd rather risk gamely
    And lose for my trying
Than grind around tamely
    —A cog in the mill.
I'd rather fail greatly
    With courage undying
Than plod on sedately
    With never a thrill!

The game's in the playing
    And, losing or winning,
The fun's in essaying
    Your bravest and best,
In taking your chances
    While Fate's wheel is spinning,
And backing your fancies
    With nerve and with zest!

Let stodgy folk censure
    And timid folk quaver,
But life sans adventure
    Is weary to bear,
The dangers we're sharing
    Give living its savour,
I'd rather die daring
    Than never to dare!

OLD STUFF

The fashion is to sneer at them, to mock and mouth and
    jeer at them,
    Those simple honest maxims that the copybooks
    contained;
For modernists most cynical look down as from a
    pinnacle
    And tell us that the potency of ancient saws has
    waned.
They damn them in totality for all their "smug
    morality."
    "Be good and you'll be happy" is, they tell us, false
    and trite,
But spite of skeptics critical and hyper-analytical
    I have a mild suspicion that the copybooks are right!

"Truth, crushed to earth, shall rise again" is proven to
    our eyes again
    If we but watch humanity about us, day by day,
And underneath Old Sol I see that Honesty's a policy
    Which, by and large and in the main, is pretty sure
    to pay;
Yes, call them "dull beatitudes and ancient, moldy
    platitudes"
    Yet somehow those who follow them keep rather near
    the light,
For simple tests and practical bear out their truth
    didactical
    And as a working plan of life the copybooks are right!

They lack in vim and snappiness but as a guide to
    happiness
    Those plain and prosy proverbs of our fathers are
    the stuff;
"The wage of sin is death" they say, and, sure as we
    draw breath, they say,
    A thing that's true as gospel—for it's proven times
    enough.

The highbrows may get gay with them but they can't
    do away with them;
    Those dry and dusty slogans will not vanish from
      our sight.
They're fusty, musty, serious; they bore us and they
    weary us
    But, take 'em all in all, my son, the copybooks are
      right!

SUCCESS

If you want a thing bad enough
To go out and fight for it,
Work day and night for it,
Give up your time and your peace and your sleep for it,
If only desire of it
Makes you quite mad enough
Never to tire of it,
Makes you hold other things tawdry and cheap for it;
If life seems all empty and useless without it
And all that you scheme and you dream is about it,
If gladly you'll sweat for it,
Fret for it,
Plan for it,
Lose all your terror of God or of man for it,
If you'll simply go after that thing that you want,
With all your capacity,
Strength and sagacity,
Faith, hope and confidence, stern pertinacity,
If neither cold poverty, famished and gaunt,
Nor sickness nor pain
Of body or brain
Can turn you away from the thing that you want,
If dogged and grim you besiege and beset it,
You'll get it!

THE BEAN

The bean!
   Say, buddy, the more I have seen,
The more do I see—and I'm putting it strong,
The bean is the thing that'll help you along.
    Yes, kiddo, you tell 'em
    The old cerebellum
Whenever you get in the strife and the tussle
Has got it all over the bone and the muscle.
You may have the shoulders and chest of an ox
But you're pretty sure to be shy on the rocks
    Unless you will use—well, you know what I mean,
           The bean!

The nut!
   The guy who don't use it's a mutt.
You will not get far if you never have shown
There's anything north of your clavicle bone;
There's many a bird who has fallen down flat
Who thought that his head was for parking his hat,
    And never would use it for anything more;
    Then wondered why luck didn't knock at his door
—There's millions of dubs who've used everything but
           The nut!

The bean!
   Just keep it well tended and keen,
And whet it with books and with knowledge worth while
And it will repay you in bountiful style.
    Your knob
    Will help you to better your job,
'Twill lessen your work and 'twill help you make good
If only you'll use it the way that you should;
    It's something you need in your play and your biz;
    The more that you use it the better it is;
It makes life successful and rich and serene,
           The bean!

ESSENTIAL

You'll never get anywhere,
    Never do anything,
        Never be any one much;
No honor or fame
    Will accrue to your name,
        You'll never have wealth in your clutch,
    Unless you go striving for,
        Doggedly driving for,
            Seeking the thing that you wish;
                How do some guys
                    Manage to rise?
Take it from me, it's
                Ambish!

Although you have cleverness,
    Brains and ability,
        Plenty of deftness and skill,
    The thing that you need
        If you hope to succeed
            Is Courage and Power of Will;
    Without pertinacity
        All your capacity
Leaves you a failure, poor fish!
    How do the Great
        Get to that state?
I've got the answer—
                Ambish!

You'll hear it called restlessness,
    Wanton irreverence,
Discontent, lunacy, too,
        But it is the force
            That alters life's course
And makes the world over anew;

The one irrepressible,
　　Strange and unguessable
Cosmic, unwavering Wish!
　　How did we climb
　　　Out of the slime?
You tell 'em, Buddy—
　　　　"Ambish!"

THE FREE COURSE

Not mine the track of a star in space
　　Which must keep to its course on high,
With never a chance for a swifter pace
　　Or a romp in the vasty sky;

Though the star be safe and the star hold true
　　I would rather be wholly free
To run amuck in the heavenly blue,
　　So—the comet's course for me,

To leap in leaps of a billion miles
　　'Mid the stars of the milky way,
And to play hop skotch through the stellar aisles
　　In a boisterous mood of play!

If I were a star I would quickly tire
　　Of a path that was fixed and tame,
And I'd whoop through space with a tail of fire
　　And burst in a flare of flame!

THE PRICE

Whatever of freedom we own
    Somebody has striven and tried for it;
By war through the years it has grown
    By strength of the men who have died for it;
Each stone in the structure of truth—
    Some one has made ready and right for it.
Some one has spent heart's blood and youth,
    Some one has been willing to fight for it.

Not always has blood been the pay
    But always a price has been paid for it;
The worth of achievement to-day
    Is gauged by the struggle we've made for it.
There need not be rancor or hate
    Nor bitterness, terror and blight for it,
But nothing is worthy or great
    Unless you are willing to fight for it.

You cannot buy progress with gold
    (You get but the emptiest shell of it);
But to win it and earn it and hold
    You must go through the heat and the hell of it,
You must suffer the sweat and the pain,
    You must toil all the day and the night for it,
For nothing worth while you can gain
    Unless you are willing to fight for it.

VERDUN

"They shall not pass!" In dug-out and in trench
   The phrase was muttered as the poilus fought.
   The earth and sky were but a shambles, fraught
With gas and bursting shells and with the drench
Of shrapnel. Yet, in all the battle-stench,
   'Mid horror heaped on horror past all thought
   The thin line stood. A miracle was wrought;
They could not break the Will that held the French.

Each human soul must meet its own Verdun
   That crisis when the armies of despair
   Attack the fortress in a serried mass;
Not by brute strength may this great fight be won,
   But only by the Will that can declare
   In face of all Hell's hosts, "They shall not pass!"

START WHERE YOU STAND

(When a man who had been in the penitentiary applied to Henry Ford for employment, he started to tell Mr. Ford his story. "Never mind," said Mr. Ford, "I don't care about the past. Start where you stand!")

Start where you stand and never mind the past,
    The past won't help you in beginning new,
If you have left it all behind at last
    Why, that's enough, you're done with it, you're
        through;
This is another chapter in the book,
    This is another race that you have planned,
Don't give the vanished days a backward look,
    Start where you stand.

The world won't care about your old defeats
    If you can start anew and win success,
The future is your time, and time is fleet
    And there is much of work and strain and stress;
Forget the buried woes and dead despairs,
    Here is a brand new trial right at hand,
The future is for him who does and dares,
    Start where you stand.

Old failures will not halt, old triumphs aid,
    To-day's the thing, to-morrow soon will be;
Get in the fight and face it, unafraid
    And leave the past to ancient history;
What has been, has been; yesterday is dead
    And by it you are neither blessed or banned,
Take courage, man, be brave and drive ahead,
    Start where you stand!

DO IT NOW

If with pleasure you are viewing any work a man is doing,
    If you like him or you love him, tell him *now!*
Don't withhold your approbation till the parson makes oration
    As he lies with snowy lilies on his brow;
For, no matter how you shout it, he won't really care about it,
    He won't know how many teardrops you may shed.
If you think some praise is due him, now's the time to slip it to him,
    For he cannot read his tombstone when he's dead!

More than fame and more than money is the comment kind and
        sunny
    And the hearty, warm approval of a friend.
For it gives to life a savor and it makes you stronger, braver,
    And it gives you heart and spirit to the end;
If he earns your praise—bestow it; if you like him, let him know it,
    Let the words of true encouragement be said;
Do not wait till life is over and he's underneath the clover
    For he cannot read his tombstone when he's dead!

INDISPENSABLE

The world is crowded with clever chaps
Who, given some work to do—*perhaps*
   Will finish the job in season;
   But who will probably stall and shirk,
Postpone, procrastinate, dodge the work
   For any old sort of reason;
But the Other Kind—they are precious few—
   Are the fellows who hop right to it
—The men who do what they say they'll do
   At the time that they say they'll do it!

Oh, the time we waste and the nerves we fray
With the folks who promise a job *to-day*
   And bring it in three days later!
There's nobody causes so much of pain
As the chap whose promise is wholly vain
   The chronic procrastinator!
How welcome then is the toiler who
   Having started a task, gets through it,
The man who does what he says he'll do
   At the time that he says he'll do it!

He may be plodding, he may be slow
But when he gets on the job, you know
   He'll finish it—on the minute;
And because he's true to his word and task,
He'll get whatever he cares to ask
   Of the world and the wealth that's in it.
Success will follow his efforts through
   He never will have to woo it—
This man who does what he says he'll do
   At the time that he says he'll do it!

THE CONQUEROR

Room for me, graybeards, room, make room!
Menace me not with your eyes of gloom;
Jostle me not from the place I seek,
For my arms are strong and your own are weak,
And if my plea to you be denied
I'll thrust your wearying forms aside.
Pity you? Yes, but I cannot stay;
I am the spirit of Youth; make way!

Room for me, timid ones, room, make room!
Little I care for your fret and fume—
I dare whatever is mine to meet,
I laugh at sorrow and jeer defeat;
To doubt and doubters I give the lie,
And fear is stilled as I swagger by,
And life's a fight and I seek the fray;
I am the spirit of Youth; make way!

Room for me, mighty ones, room, make room!
I fear no power and dread no doom;
And you who curse me or you who bless
Alike must bow to my dauntlessness.
I topple the king from his golden throne,
I smash old idols of brass and stone,
I am not hampered by yesterday.
Room for the spirit of Youth; make way!

Room for me, all of you, make me room!
Where the rifles crash and the cannon boom,
Where glory beckons or love or fame
I plunge me heedlessly in the game.
The old, the wary, the wise, the great,
They cannot stay me, for I am Fate,
The brave young master of all good play,
I am the spirit of Youth; make way!

THE ANGRY ONES

("When we were angry, and young and happy."

CHESTERTON)

They are the smashers of harsh traditions,
    They are the breakers of idols vain,
The angry men with a raging mission,
    With furious heart and with seething brain.
For their souls are thrilled with a splendid ire
    At Mammon throned and at Man cast down,
And their eyes are baleful with angry fire
    And they wear their rage as a flaming crown!

They cannot view with a calm quiescent
    The sight of ancient established wrongs,
They fight with a wrath that is incandescent,
    And march to the battle with angry songs!
They do not hate in a half-way fashion
    The mercenaries of craft and greed,
But wield their weapons in righteous passion—
    Crusaders come of a fighting breed.

Oh, it is a clean white rage which quickens
    The struggle upward to better things,
They are joyously mad when the conflict thickens,
    Their anger giveth their spirit wings;
Theirs is the wrath that at last shall leaven
    The soul of man till it breaks the clod,
A glorious fury straight from heaven,
    A thunderbolt from the hand of God!

SPURS

My foes, they are my dearest friends;
    They save me from placidity;
They free my life, its aims and ends,
    Of sloth and pale vapidity;
They wake me from my dullest doze
    And force me to my job again;
They keep me always on my toes,
    Alive, alert, athrob again!

My foes! They jeer my smug conceit,
    Which I am fondly nourishing;
They chasten me with loss, defeat,
    When luck becomes too flourishing.
I dare not halt in my advance
    Or shirk things with impunity;
My foes would see in such a chance
    A golden opportunity.

My friends—the debt to them is great;
    Their love and faith I'm treasuring,
But it's my foes who hold me straight
    And help me past all measuring;
They keep me always "in the pink."
    A stimulant their venom is,
Which makes me strong and "fit." I drink
    A health unto mine enemies!

THE MILLENNIUM

(Apologies as Usual)

When earth's last evil is righted, and earth's last sinner reformed,
When all of the graft is ended, when sin's last fortress is stormed,
We shall rest for an age or longer and gaze with a happy smile
On the work that we have accomplished—a world that is void
    of guile,
But when the resting is over and we start on the job anew,
What will be left for the doing, and what in the world will we do?

There will be no sorrows to lighten, no poverty, crime or pain,
No greedy robbers to battle, no octopus to be slain,
And those who were ever foremost in fighting the goodly fight
Will find no foemen to grapple and never a wrong to right,
A mood of perfect contentment the heart of the world will lull
And each of us will be happy—and Lord! but it will be dull!

When earth's last evil is righted—I hope I shall not be there;
I should long for the old-time conflict, for the work and worry
    and care,
There's fun in the bitter fighting, there's joy in the mighty game
Of battling against the forces of evil and woe and shame.
You may long for the perfect era, but I'm for the clash and jar,
The shouts and the cheers and the tumult in a world of Things as
    They Are!

PRAYER OF A SPORTSMAN

Dear Lord, in the battle that goes on through life
    I ask but a field that is fair,
A chance that is equal with all in the strife,
    A courage to strive and to dare;
And if I should win, let it be by the code
    With my faith and my honor held high;
And if I should lose, let me stand by the road
    And cheer as the winners go by!

And Lord, may my shouts be ungrudging and clear,
    A tribute that comes from the heart,
And let me not cherish a snarl or a sneer
    Or play any sniveling part;
Let me say: "There they ride on whom laurel's bestowed
    Since they played the game better than I,"
Let me stand with a smile by the side of the road
    And cheer as the winners go by!

So grant me to conquer, if conquer I can
    By proving my worth in the fray;
But teach me to lose like a Regular Man
    And not like a craven, I pray.
Let me take off my hat to the warriors who strode
    To victory splendid and high,
Yea, teach me to stand by the side of the road
    And cheer as the winners go by!

THE CONTINUOUS PERFORMANCE

*("You keep on going—maybe you can't go much, but
you do go a little."*

From Booth Tarkington's *Alice Adams.)*

It isn't fun when your hopes seem finished
    And all your visions have come to naught,
When your youth is gone and your strength diminished
    And broken all of the dreams you've sought.
It isn't fun when your projects splendid,
    Your castles in Spain all glad and glowing,
Crash down to ruin that can't be mended,
    Yet, somehow or other, you keep on going!

It isn't fun when you know the glamour
    Is gone from life, and little remains
But dull reality, dust and clamor,
    And puny triumphs and plodding gains.
When life is a muddle of sad confusions,
    A tangled puzzle beyond all knowing,
A mess of tarnished and cheap illusions—
    Yet somehow or other you keep on going!

It seems no use, but you just keep plodding
    Through force of habit; and then, and then—
You suddenly notice the flowers nodding
    Along the side of the road again.
Though nevermore shall the hours be giving
    The thrill you knew of the past's bestowing,
You'll come again to a zest in living
    If somehow or other you keep on going!

THE FAILURES

The hills are bare of verdure, the valleys clogged with snow,
And winds of bitter winter sweep howling to and fro;
The roads that lured us strongly are drifted, deep and white,
And peaks that seemed to beckon are hidden from our sight;
The sun, who used to call us, in merry comradewise,
Now glowers, dull and sullen, from gray and sodden skies;
The sea is black and angry and flecked with cruel foam,
Too long, too long we tarried, and now—we stay at home.

We talked of wondrous ventures, our tongues would never tire,
Yet we of scanty courage sit close before the fire,
We cringe to hear the shrieking of blasts that stab and fleer,
We stir the coals and whisper, "Thank God that we are here!"
Somewhere the vagrant pilgrims are on the open way,
Unmindful of to-morrow and careless of to-day;
And though WE drudge or dawdle and seek to sink our shame,
We know our souls are little—we feared to risk the Game.

We talked of "joyous freedom"—but thought, with quaking
    knees,
Of hardships and of perils on distant roads and seas;
We babbled light of hunger—and gripped, with clutching
    hands,
The gold great-hearted rovers had wrested from the sands.
What need is there to mumble of "reasons," you and I?
We lingered, lingered, lingered, because we feared to try;
And though our fortunes flourish, and fame shall heed our call,
We'll know ourselves for failures and cowards after all!

BOTTOMS UP!

(*"Every now and then I like to drink the wine of life—with brandy in it!"*—Letter of Theodore Roosevelt to Senator Lodge.)

The Wine of Life!—Most men prefer
    A vintage bland and smooth and mild,
Something to make their pulses purr
    With soft enchantment undefiled;
But now and then one stalks along
    Whose thirst grows mightier by the minute,
Who takes his tipple, hot and strong,
    The Wine of Life—with Brandy in it!

Where ordinary folk desire
    Life to be like a watered claret,
These topers call for liquid fire
    And with their lusty fellows share it.
In every row with Destiny
    They are the fellows who begin it,
Guzzling like Vikings, bold and free
    The Wine of Life—with Brandy in it!

They swagger to the Bar of Fate
    And slap their roll upon the bar
Demanding singeing distillate
    Fit for the hardy souls they are;
They take their potent potion neat
    And scorn with ice or fizz to thin it.
Only one mixture they find sweet—
    The Wine of Life—with Brandy in it!

Fighters and gamesters, pioneers,
    Whose taste is spoiled for milder things,
Who rollick down the roaring years
    Swigging of life that sears and stings!
And we—we watch them, and we think
    "They drink too deep, we're all agin' it!"
—Yet wish WE had the verve to drink
    "The Wine of Life—with Brandy in it!"

TRIBUTE

He was a big man, fellows,
　　And lived as a big man should,
He was five feet six in his stocking feet
　　But let it be understood
He was six feet five in the soul of him
And all fine metal, the whole of him.

Yes, "big" is the word that fits him,
　　For only his frame was small,
There was nothing little and nothing mean
　　In the heart of his heart, at all;
He met with a smile what came to him
And life was a great big game to him.

He held himself to a standard
　　A code that was clean and high,
But looked on the failings of others
　　With a tolerant, kindly eye;
Though again and again deceived in them,
He loved his friends—and believed in them.

He never was out for trouble
　　Yet when there was need to fight,
He fought to the last ounce in him
　　For what he believed was right,
Winning, he scarcely spoke of it;
Losing, he made a joke of it.

For he was a big man, fellows,
　　And when I am lifeless clay,
I'd like to think you could look on me
　　As you do on him, and say,
"A man's brave soul was expressed in him
He was Big—and true to the best in him!"

AN IDEAL

I wish I were as trig a man,
   As big a man,
      As bright a man;
I wish I were as *right* a man in all this earthly show,
      As broad and high and long a man,
         As strong a man,
            As fine a man,
As pretty near divine a man as one I used to know.

      I wish I were as grave a man,
         As brave a man,
            As keen a man,
As learned and serene a man, as fair to friend and foe.
         I wish I owned sagaciousness
            And graciousness
               As should a man
Who hopes to be as good a man as one I used to know.

      I'd be a creature glorious,
         Victorious,
            A Wonder-man,
Not just a sort of Blunder-man whose ways and thoughts
      are slow.
         If I could only be the man,
            One-tenth of one degree the man,
I used to think my father was when I was ten or so.

FRESH EVERY HOUR

Election promises, glibly spoken,
Are easily made—and easily broken.

They're frail and fragile and slightly brittle,
So why complain if they crack a little?

The promise made was a cut in taxes,
And every moment the burden waxes;

We won't be harsh in the way we judge it,
But where, oh where is the balanced budget?

And, 'spite of promises, officeholders
Are twice as heavy upon our shoulders.

But why be sore at a broken promise?
The Powers that be can always calm us,

And when one promise has cracked in two
They'll give us another that's nice and new!

New York American, May 9, 1936:

Andrew Fletcher wrote in a letter to the Marquis of Montrose more than three hundred years ago about a sage who believed that if a man were permitted to make all the ballads of a country he need not care who made the laws.

THE PROFITS AND LOSS

When "planned economy" first began
    It looked like a swell "idee"—
Until we learned that it had no plan
    And wasn't economee.

For the taxes rise and the budget's shot
    And the New Deal costs are met
By spending money we haven't got
    For things that we never get.

The billions roll in a mighty stream,
    A regular tidal flood,
With the net result that each spending scheme
    Bogs down in a sea of mud.

When plans and programs go all to pot
    Do the New Deal planners fret?
Why no, they think up a brand new lot
Of schemes to spend what we haven't got
    For things we will never get!

EVEN STEVEN

*(Surveys show that in many industries the annual
tax-bill equals the payroll.)*

A dollar for the workingman
    For hard, productive work—
(And a dollar for the wages
    Of a Governmental clerk!)

A dollar for the artisan
    Who keeps his job in shape—
(And a dollar for the bureaucrat
    All tangled up in tape!)

A dollar for the labor
    Of the builder and erector—
(And a dollar for the pockets
    Of the revenue collector!)

A dollar for the services
    A true producer renders—
(And a dollar for experiments
    Of Governmental spenders!)

A dollar for the earners
    And the savers and the thrifty—
(And a dollar for the wasters,
    It's a case of fifty-fifty!)

And we wonder why we stagger
    With this burden on our backs
Of a dollar paid for labor
    And a dollar paid for tax!

JUST ANOTHER STRAW

(New Dealers Plan Heavier Taxes)

Giddy-yup, Camel, and show no discontent—
The Business of a Nation is all you represent;
There's twenty different drivers to make you "gee"
   and "haw,"
But, Giddy-yup, Camel! (And here's another straw!)

Giddy-yup, Camel! You bear a heavy load
For rough, tough going on a long hard road;
Your legs are weary and your back is raw,
But, Giddy-yup, Camel! (And here's another straw!)

Giddy-yup, Camel! You've got a heavy load,
Hackled by restrictions and shackled by a Code;
Each step is regulated by a brand new law,
But, Giddy-yup, Camel! (And here's another straw!)

Giddy-yup, Camel! You stagger on your track.
(What cargo can be carried on a camel's back?)
You bear the greatest burden that we ever saw,
But, Giddy-yup, Camel! (And here's another straw!)

ANNIE UP TO DATE

(With the usual apologies)

If Little Orphant Annie were to come around today
And mix a bit in politics, she probably would say:
"The Bureaucrats in Washington are busy spending money
On schemes to make the country flow with Grade-A milk
    and honey.
And though their vast experiments have mostly boggled
    down,
You mustn't say, 'I told you so!' You mustn't laugh or frown,
You mustn't say the taxes and the debts are growing great
Or you'll be called a brigand and a menace to the State!
So, do as the professors say, and don't show any doubt
Or the Bureaucrats'll git you
                    Ef you
              Don't
                      Watch
                          Out!

"For instance, onc't a business man had made a little profit,
And said the New Deal didn't help—he even dared to scoff it!
And then—he was descended on by Bureaucrats in hordes
And tried before commissions and investigating boards;
They tied him up with rulings by the dozen and the score,
They sued him on his income back to 1894,
And jailed him under statutes that nobody knew about,
For the Bureaucrats'll git you
                    Ef you
              Don't
                      Watch
                          Out!

"So do not utter any but constructive criticism,
And cheer for Rex and Felix and hooray for Farleyism,
And live the more abundant life that comes from I.O.U.'s,
And let the all-wise Bureaucrats instruct you in your views,
And let them regiment your life according to a plan,

For rugged individuals are underneath the ban.
So be a docile robot and a humble, spineless lout,
Or the Bureaucrats'll git you
                            Ef you
                        Don't
                            Watch
                                Out!"

COUNTER-CONVOLUTION

We pay the truckman *not* to raise
            Tomatoes;
We pay the stockman *not* to graze
            His cows;
We pay the farmer *not* to sow
            Potatoes;
And other farmers *not* to grow
            Their sows!

Such is the plan of Pundits and
            Professors;
It doesn't work as it was planned
            To do;
But though these Planners prove to be
            Bad guessers,
They've always got a new "idee"
            Or two!

So here's a scheme that ought to aid
            The nation,
A little Plan that would evade
            Red Ink!
Let's take a tip from this
            Administration
And pay the Brain-Trust Thinkers
            NOT to think!

73

JUST SUPPOSE

Suppose we cease for a while to pan
The mind of the Practical Business Man;
    Suppose we say,
    In a practical way:
"He isn't perfect, but in the main,
Through all the worry and stress and strain,
He's pretty well managed, without a yelp,
To keep things going and pay his help.
So—there may be room in the cosmic plan
For the mind of the Practical Business Man!"

Suppose we say as we calmly scan
The work of the Practical Business Man:
    "In a world that's real,
    And not ideal,
He's faced conditions as best he could,
With brains and moderate hardihood;
He hasn't hit one hundred per cent.
(But neither, my dears, has the Government.)
So maybe we shouldn't *always* tan
The hide of the Practical Business Man."

Suppose we say: "He's a decent scout,
Trying to figure the best way out,
Asking no odds, though the game is tough,
But a reasonable chance to '*do his stuff.*' "
Suppose we give him that chance, instead
Of tripping him up when he starts ahead?
We might discover Good Times began
In the mind of the Practical Business Man!

JUST ANTI-SOCIAL

We've loaded him with a lot of taxes
    And rules and codes—but there's something funny;
In spite of the way his burden waxes
    The son-of-a-gun is making money!

Whenever he's given a boost to trade
    We've taken an extra tribute off it,
But still the villain is undismayed,
    The son-of-a-gun has shown a Profit!

We grind out daily a brand new grist
    Of regulations by Profs. and scholars,
But the Rugged Individualist
    Is still producing some surplus dollars!

We've frowned on personal, private gains,
    As most immoral, and due for censure,
But the son-of-a-gun with Business Brains
    Continues risking some new adventure!

In spite of Planners and New Deal sages
    With Communistical dreams and yearnings,
This Capitalistic guy pays wages,
    And SOME of his stocks and bonds show earnings!

We've moved the bases, and changed the lines,
    And altered the rules for every inning,
With added penalties, doubled fines,
    But the son-of-a-gun insists on winning!

It's anti-social to fail to fail,
    It makes our wonderful schemes look funny;
Rush the Traitor at once to jail,
    For the son-of-a-gun is making money!

THE LITTLE TIN GODS

(Washington Cracks Down on Anti-New Deal
Governors—Headline)

If you want to keep your "Place in the Sun"
With the Little Tin Gods in Washington
You must "be 'umble" and doff your hat
To the merest whim of a bureaucrat.
If you dig a tunnel under a ridge,
Build a highway or stretch a bridge,
You must bow to the slightest opiniyun
Of the Little Tin Gods in Washington!

You mustn't question a thing that's done
By the Little Tin Gods in Washington,
Who handle the Scheme of Things entire
And tell you whom you can hire and fire,
Reward the Sheep with a rich resplendence
And make a Goat of the Independents;
If you are not meek you will get no "mon"
From the Little Tin Gods in Washington!

In the days of old, when our souls were free,
We called such arrogance "Tyranny,"
And now—describe it as what you will,
By any name—it is Tyranny still!
To be fought with ridicule, laughter, wit,
With gallant courage and dogged grit,
Till we rip in tatters the web that's spun
By the Little Tin Gods in Washington!

JACK LONDON

An Appreciation

Here's to you, Jack, whose virile pen
    Concerns itself with Man's Size Men;
Here's to you, Jack, whose stories thrill
    With savor of the western breeze,
With magic of the south—and chill
    Shrill winds from icy floes and seas;
You have not wallowed in the mire
And muck of tales of foul desire,
For, though you've sung of fight and fraud,
    Of love and hate—ashore, afloat—
    You have not struck a ribald note
Nor made your art a common bawd.

Here's to you, Jack; I've loved your best,
    Your finest stories from the first,
Your sagas of the north and west—
    But what is more—I've loved your worst!
For, in the poorest work you do,
There's something clean and strong and true,
A tang of big and primal things,
    A sweep of forces vast and free,
A touch of wizardry which brings
    The glamour of the wild to me.

So when I read a London tale
Forthwith I'm set upon a trail
Of great enchantment, and I track
Adventure round the world and back,
With you for guide—here's to you, Jack.

TO BOOTH TARKINGTON, MASTER PENMAN

Tarkington, how shall we carol the worth of you,
  Master of marvelous magical prose?
How shall we sing of the humor and mirth of you?
  How shall we warble the art you disclose?
You who have stirred us to love or frivolity,
  Wound us up tight in your magical snare,
You who have written of plain folks and "quality,"
  Cherry and Penrod and Monsieur Beaucaire?

"Will o' the Wisp, with a flicker of Puck in you,"
  Thus warbled Hovey of Barney McGee.
Sure you have all of his charm and good luck in you,
  Mixed with a genius dazzling to see,
Love and philosophy, wisdom and joy in you;
  All these we know, but we love most of all
Just the unquenchable spirit of Boy in you,
  Blithe with the days that we'd like to recall.

You haven't dug in the muck of society
  Seeking for filth to be shown us as "Life,"
Yet you have pictured in flashing variety
  Tragedy, comedy, glamour and strife;
Here's to you, Tarkington, Humanitarian,
  Humanist, rather, with eyes that are clear;
May you live long as a hale centenarian,
  Writing more bully good tales every year!

TO DOUG.

Most of the movie folk fill me with weariness,
    Most of the films are a horrible bore,
Chaplin instils me with feelings of dreariness,
    Arbuckle thrills me with thirst for his gore;
Yet when I notice the placards that feature you
    I join the line, like the veriest bug,
How can I help it, you blithe, healthy creature, you,
        Doug!

You are the spirit of Pan at his happiest
    You are a faun that is brought up to date,
You are the huskiest, liveliest, snappiest
    Picture of youth in its joyous estate;
Huge are the sums that the gossips are saying you
    Add every day to your bank account snug;
Well, you're worth more than whatever they're paying
    you,
        Doug!

Why, just your smile—who can figure the worth of it?
    Leaping so boyishly out of the screen,
All of the whimsical, magical mirth of it
    Welling up fresh from a heart that is clean,
You're like a breeze with the tang of the west to it,
    Ever a tonic and never a drug,
You bring romance with a glorious zest to it,
        Doug!

CHAPLIN SATIETY

Published in the Detroit, Michigan *Free Press*, October 15, 1915:

Hear! Hear! Likewise Hurrah!

Berton Braley, poet, humorist, satirist and puncturer of pretense in general, writes in the November Green Book Magazine these lines, which will find a double-emphasis echo in millions of human hearts:

Charlie, old pal, we've no personal peeve at you—
    None, anyhow, we at present recall;
Yet we are looking for something to heave at you—
    Paving-brick, building stone, hammer or maul.
Charlie, we're weary of every old trick of you—
    Bored with your face and your mustache and cane.
Gosh, but we've seen you so much we are sick of you;
    Charlie, we're breaking down under the strain!

You've been exhibited, touted and pageanted,
    Billboarded, placarded hither and yon.
Never was anyone half so press-agented;
    Go where we will we must happen upon
Busts of you, statuettes, photographs various,
    Cartoons and comments and posters galore;
Honestly, Charlie, in ways multifarious
    You're getting more of a spread than the war!

Vaudeville's crowded with acts imitating you;
    Every old movie has you on the screen.
We who were strong for you soon will be hating you
    Simply because you're so constantly seen.
Granted you're gifted with vim and agility;
    Granted you're there with the pep and the zest;
Yet, ere you drive us to dull imbecility,
    Charlie we beg of you—give us a rest!

GUESS WHO?

Sometimes fantastical,
Often bombastical,
Always dynamic and never scholastical,
   Slightly uproarious,
   Bracing as Boreas,
Living each day with a zest that is glorious,
Bane of the highbrows and folk hypercritical,
   Subject of many a plutocrat's curse,
Buried in state by his foemen political
   Only to climb up and pilot the hearse!

There is an air to him,
There's such a flare to him,
There's such a rare, debonair do-and-dare to him!
   Bull dog tenacity,
   Mixed with vivacity,
Tempered with humor and sense and sagacity;
What if his speeches are crowded with platitudes,
   Somehow he's built on the popular plan,
Actions and manner and sayings and attitudes,
   All of them prove him a Regular Man!

Quite undistressable,
Most irrepressible,
Open and frank—yet a problem unguessable,
   Terse, though didactical,
   Learned, but practical,
Strong for preparedness, moral and tactical,
Vivid and vital and vervy and vigorous,
   Simply and humanly "playing the game,"
Preaching and living a life that is rigorous,
   ——Give you three guesses to call him by name!*

*Editor's Guess: Teddy Roosevelt

SONNETS OF SEVEN CITIES

I

NEW ORLEANS

Dark, languorous, with heavy lidded eyes
   That glow and smolder with a constant fire,
   She stirs men's hearts with glorious desire
By glances turned upon them waywardwise;
She is incarnate carnival, she plies
   Her cavaliers with wine of mystery,
Under her mask they know not what there lies,
   But linger, rapt, enchanted, till they see.

No disillusion greets them when she lifts
   That dainty mask, for she is fair and kind.
But take her not for one who idly drifts
   Through lazy days with purpose undesigned
For though her eyes are warm, and warm her lips,
Her brain is building towers, ports and ships!

II

BOSTON

A lady somewhat dowdy as to dress,
   A gentle Brahmin of old family
   Sighing in shocked bewilderment to see
How progress threatens her exclusiveness;
She shows a helpless, fluttering distress
   Because her children somehow seem to be
   Raucously modern, wholly out of key
With what she feels true culture should express.

And yet for all her well-bred scorn of change
　　And chill defense of custom and of caste,
Her stern resistance to the new and strange,
　　This fine old gentlewoman of the past
Has eyes whose glance, with courteous manner met,
Glows sweetly through her often raised lorgnette.

III

CHICAGO

Deep bosomed, buxom, at first glance, mature
　　Yet but a girl who wears a woman's form,
　　A willful girl whose brain is all aswarm
With dreams and doubts, thoughts vivid and obscure.
Sometimes the siren with a subtle lure
　　Her beauty ripe, seductive, richly warm;
　　Sometimes the slattern with her house a storm
Of dirt and clutter painful to endure.

She sees herself as grown to womanhood,
　　The world views her as adolescent still,
Whereat she stamps her feet—as children would—
　　And sounds her protest, angry, sharp and shrill.
But when the need is great her soul can rise
To heights of labor, love and sacrifice.

IV

PHILADELPHIA

She sits in Quaker garb and seems to drowse,
　　A plump, smug lady, with a placid air;
　　You can't imagine roses in her hair
Or sparkling eyes beneath those level brows.
But whisper to her of a gay carouse
　　She'll doff her cloak and on your vision flare
　　White shouldered, scarlet clad, enticing, fair,
Wide eyed and pagan as the law allows.

Her domicile is prim, immaculate
    (That part of it which faces on the street)
But in the rear you find a doubtful state,
    Cigar butts, bottles, marks of dirty feet,
Where thieves and grafters hold rough carnival
While she pretends they are not there at all.

V

SAN FRANCISCO

High-colored, sparkling, very much alive,
    Her feet atingle ever for a dance,
    Her eyes agleam with laughter and romance
Her brain alert to vision and contrive,
Gayly she greets what fortune may arrive
    Fearless of any turn of circumstance;
    Gives destiny a bright, flirtatious glance
And fate a wink—nor cares how they connive.

She jazzes to the music of the spheres
    And then—'twixt dance and dance—with sudden thought,
She stops to fashion miracles; the years
    Will look with wonder on the dreams she wrought.
And she smiles blithely on her work, and then
Her syncopating feet dance on again!

VI

PITTSBURGH

A factory girl with smudges on her cheek
    And strong hands hardened with her daily toil
    Where furnaces flare forth and caldrons boil
With white hot metal, and the steel shears shriek;
This is no sheltered maiden, soft and meek,
    But one who dares the labor and the moil
    To change the ore and coal ripped from the soil
Into the tools of progress that men seek.

Yet she has softer hours when, silken clad,
　　She seeks the lights and laughs the night away,
Wasting her wages like a spendthrift glad,
　　Avid of pleasure and of love and play;
But though her beauty glows at such a time
She cannot wholly free her hands of grime.

VII

NEW YORK

Her mouth is carmine and her cheeks too red,
　　Her eyes too bright and hard; her garb is smart,
　　The product of sophisticated art
From shoes to that confection on her head.
Worship is daily food that she is fed,
　　It thrills her not, nor seems to warm her heart,
　　She takes her royal way through street and mart
Brilliant, and proud, as to the purple bred.

And so men say that she is hard as steel
　　Not sensing that her paint, her calm disdain
　　　　Are but the trappings of the rôle she plays,
And that to lovers true she will reveal
　　Love, comradeship, and sympathy to pain,
　　　　Faith that endures and loyalty that stays!

NEWARK—THE BUILDER

*(This poem won one of the Prizes at the Newark
Anniversary Celebration, 1917.)*

Never a jungle is penetrated,
   Never an unknown sea is dared,
Never adventure is consummated,
   Never a faint new trail is fared,
But that some dreamer has had the vision
   Which leads men on to the ends of earth,
That laughs at doubting and scorns derision
   And falters not at the cynic's mirth.

So the dreamer dreams, but there follows after
   The mighty epic of steel and stone,
When caisson, scaffold and wall and rafter
   Have made a fact where the dream was shown,
And so with furnace and lathe and hammer,
   With blast that rumbles and shaft that gleams,
Her factories crowned with a grimy glamor
   Newark buildeth the dreamer's dreams.

Where the torrent leaps with a roar of thunder,
   Where the bridge is built or the dam is laid,
Where the wet walled tunnel burrows under
   Mountain, river and palisade,
There is Newark's magic of nail or girder,
   Of spikes and castings and posts and beams,
The needs and wants of the world have spurred her
   Newark—city that builds our dreams.

She has fashioned tools for the world's rough duty,
   For the men that dig and the men that hew,
She has fashioned jewels for wealth and beauty,
   She has shod the prince and the pauper, too.
Yes, the dreamer dreams, he's the wonder waker,
   With soul that hungers and brain that teems,
But back of him toils the magic maker,
   Newark—city that builds his dreams.

WHERE EVERYBODY HAS A HORN TO TOOT

—Los Angeles

Los Angeles, the glamorous, where all the streets are clamorous
    With motor cars too numerous to count;
Where real-estators trot to you to sell a house and lot to you,
    And population's always on the mount.
Los Angeles, where baby-talk quite naturally may be talk
    Of oil and mines and railway lines and fruit;
A feverishly busy town, a tonic and a fizzy town,
    Where everybody has a horn to toot.

Los Angeles, where roses are, yet where the people's noses are
    Sometimes assailed with oil and sooty smoke;
Where one may quickly cop a roll and just as swiftly drop a roll,
    Be rich today—tomorrow wholly broke!
A proud, enthusiastic town, at times a bit bombastic town,
    Whose boosters boost by night as well as day.
A town that has society of every known variety
    And every game on earth for them to play!

Los Angeles, where folly would appear to reign at Hollywood
    (If you believe the tales that people spread),
But where the movie-makers are as decorous as Quakers are
    Who labor, play a bit, and go to bed.
(Whichever tale seems best to you of these that I've expressed to you,
    Accept it, doubtless neither one is right—
You know how rumors tangle us—and I've observed Los Angeles
    From three one afternoon till ten at night!)

A GOTHAMITE IN CAMELOT

Now James H. Brown in Gotham Town
    Did live and work and play.
Away from there he'd seldom fare
    And almost never stray.

Most commonplace in form and face
    Our hero was, I wot,
Till, on a time, he dreamed he was
    A Knight in Camelot.

He had a helmet on his head
    And armor round his form
Of iron wrought—the which, he thought
    Uncomfortably warm.

"What's this," he cried, "that I'm inside,
    And what's this mast I hold?"
(It was a lance; his ignorance
    Is fearful to behold.)

His lackey spoke: "Sire, gentlefolk
    On these things place reliance
For jousts with knights and sundry fights
    With ogres, dragons, giants!"

Then with a frown spake James H. Brown,
    "All right, kid, lead me to it,
This knightly stuff sounds kind of rough
    But maybe I can do it!"

So James H. Brown began to tilt
    And in a manner breezy
He dodged each blow, then tripped his foe
    And chuckled, "This is easy!"

The dragons too, he blithely slew
  And giants, fierce and dread ones,
While ogres grim were pie for him;
  He strewed the land with dead ones.

When Merlin pulled his magic tricks
  Our hero sneered, "A greeny
Could get that guy with half an eye
  You otta see Houdini!"

Said Launcelot, "Brave warrior, what
  Has been your early training
That you are now so great a wow?
  I vow it takes explaining!"

Said James H. Brown, "In Gotham Town
  I joust each day, I bet you,
With busses, autos, ten-ton trucks;
  If you ain't quick—they get you!

"Your Giants—poor! They're amatoor,
  They do things in a dub way;
Say, listen Pard, I'VE bucked a Guard
  At rush hour in the Subway!

"Your dragons and your ogres—say,
  They're meek and limp and waxy;
I'VE bluffed the door-man at the Ritz,
  The Chauffeur of a Taxi;

"I'VE made box-office clerks be good,
  I'VE bawled out swell Head-Waiters,
I'VE made the Janitor send steam
  Through ice-cold radiators!

"I'm going back to New York Town
  Where life has more attraction,
This Camelot is not so hot,
  I want a little action!"

And James H. Brown of Gotham Town
  When these here words were spoken
Found he was not in Camelot
  But that he had awoken!

DIMENSIONS

Broad smiles that flash at sight of cash,
  Broad bursts of light high up in air,
Broad walks packed tight by day and night,
  Broad-backed policemen here and there;

Broad palms that itch for tribute rich
  From broadcloth garb with money in it,
Broad matrons viewed absorbing food
  And getting broader every minute;

Broad streams of those whose looks disclose
  They came across the broad pray-raries
To dance and dine where white lights shine
  And gaze upon the merry-merries.

Broad tales that win a broader grin
  From those who listen, quite unawed;
Broad signs that leer to bid you hear
  Broad farces brought in from abroad:

Broad jokes that make the midriff quake,
  Broad robberies at broad of day,
Broad fake, broad bluff, broad tragic stuff,
  Broad comedy—Broadway!

BY DEGREES

I make a very modest plea
To which I hope you will agree;
    I'm in no rush
    To make you blush
At my affection hot;
But, love me now a little bit;
To-morrow add a bit to it
And as the days proceed to flit,
    You'll love me quite a lot.

Your maiden doubts I would not press
By begging for a sweet caress;
    I'll give you time
    To learn that I'm
A patient chap, I wot;
But—kiss me now a little bit,
To-morrow more, if you see fit,
And after you are used to it
    You'll kiss me quite a lot.

I know it isn't in your head
That I'm the man you want to wed,
    But still you ought
    To give it thought,
Although it seems absurd;
So—think of it a little bit.
To-morrow give more thought to it,
And as the days proceed to flit
    Perhaps you'll say the word.

NEGATION

Dear Lady, I don't mind admitting to you
    That my heart greatly trembled and shook at
The first time you happened to come to my view,
    You were awfully hard not to look at!

Your manner was modest, I know that it was,
    But your eyes were so brightly alert with
Sheer fun, that I flirted a little because
    You truly were hard not to flirt with.

Then later acquaintance proved this very plain
    Which all who have known you agree with,
To get on without you was sorrow and pain;
    You were terribly hard not to *be* with.

So though I have struggled to keep my heart whole
    It seems to be useless, and therefore,
I've fallen in love with you, body and soul,
    You are frightfully hard not to care for.

I'd resolved I'd remain in a bachelor's state,
    I thought I was cautious and wary,
Yet I march to the altar with manner elate,
    You're impossibly hard not to marry!

ANY LOVER TO HIS LASS

Most people live a humdrum life
    When they are married; day by day
They have their petty little strife,
    They fuss and argue, yea and nay.
    And so they wear their lives away;
But we, we gaze in scorn thereat
    And in our confidence we say:
"Ah, *we* won't ever be like that!"

Many a husband leaves his wife
    While he goes out alone to play;
A shrew whose tongue is like a knife
    Makes many a spouse grow dour and gray.
    While love that once was blithe and gay
Grows unromantic, bald and fat;
    But *our* love never shall decay
And *we* won't ever be like that!

Shrill as the note of any fife
    The cynics' voices warn us, "Stay!
The matrimonial state is rife
    With trouble, worry and dismay;
    Marriage is one continual fray
Or else a boredom, dull and flat!"
    But why should that concern *us*, pray?
For we won't *ever* be like that!

ENVOY

Sweetheart, though all the world should flay
    Wedlock as one continual spat;
It wouldn't cause us to delay
    For we won't ever be like that!

TO "THE WIFE"

You say I'm "getting used" to you,
That where I once enthused to you,
Regarding all your loveliness enchanted,
I now accept it prosily
And cease to paint it rosily,
In brief, you say I'm taking you for granted!

Your charges made so tearfully
Are here admitted cheerfully.
No shame or guilt my snowy brow is wreathing.
For you've become a part of me,
The very soul and heart of me.
I'm used to you—as I am used to breathing.

I'm used to you, as, steadily,
I'm used to counting readily
Upon my heart to keep my pulses going;
I'm used to you—as flowers to
The sunshine and the showers too;
Or trees are used to sap that keeps them growing.

I'm used to you—each way of you,
The moods both sad and gay of you.
I'm used to you—to everything about you;
I'm used to you; that's shown to be
A fact. Yes, I have grown to be
So used to you I couldn't live without you!

THE ADDED INGREDIENT

Builder, make me a house,
    Giving your skill and care to it,
Build it sturdy and strong
    With comfort and warmth and wear to it.

Builder, make me a house
    With all of your wisest thought in it,
With some of the hopes you've known
    And some of the dreams you've sought in it.

Build it the best you know
    From roof to the basement loam of it,
And I will find me a girl
    And *she* will make me a home of it!

THE MODERN VERSION

(To a Lucy Stoner)

Stay by yourself and be my love!
We will not ape the turtledove

And live within one tiny cot
As is the common married lot.

Such humdrum ways we view amiss,
We seek a freer sort of bliss.

You keep your flat and I'll keep mine
Save that together we will dine

Say once a week. But otherwise
Our quondam freedom we will prize.

Upon your time I'll make no claim,
You'll keep your job, your maiden name,

And folks who come around to call
Will never know we're wed at all.

Stay by yourself and be my bride,
And our expenses we'll divide,

Retaining all our love's resplendence
Through Economic Independence.

And should a baby come to us
(It has been known to happen thus),

We'll shake the dice or match to see
Whether it's named for you or me.

And thus we'll live our whole lives through
Two hearts and souls—remaining two!

If with this plan you coincide,
Stay by yourself and be my bride!

THE MIRACLE

Out of a reeking tenement she trips,
    Dainty and slim and delicately fair:
Her cheeks are rose, and rose-red are her lips,
    She is a flower, grown in tainted air;
    You can't believe she could have flourished there,
Where even noonday sun is in eclipse,
    Where grim reality the glamour strips
From all life's dreams and leaves them stark and bare.

Yet here she is, a flower lush and sweet,
    That throve, somehow, in rank and fetid soil;
Young maidenhood, with light and lilting feet,
    And eyes which disillusion cannot spoil;
And—miracle which few can understand—
There are a million like her in the land!

IN THE KING'S ENGLISH

Er—Dear, and all that sort of rot,
   I'm fairly hipped about you.
I mean to say that though I've got
   Along, so far, without you,
You've bowled me over, knocked me flat,
   The good old heart is skipping.
In fact I think you'll gather that
   I think you're simply ripping!

Your form, your eyes, your lips, your hair
   Are—er—top hole. Yes, quite so.
I mean to say you have an air
   That's bally well all right; so
If you should care for me, old thing,
   I'd chuck the melancholy,
And like some silly bird I'd sing
   And be distinctly jolly.

What say? Let's toddle up the aisle
   And face the good old altar.
I'm somewhat on the faithful style
   That doesn't funk or falter.
I have the oof to pay the rent
   For some—er—sylvan cot;
Right ho? Good Egg. We'll be content
   In jolly bliss. Eh, what?

THE ATAVISTIC MAID

Listen, Sweetheart, to my plea;
  Cut this highly cultured game.
All this fine gentility
  Grows to be exceeding tame.
What *I* want is low-brow love,
  Heavy, knockdown cave-man stuff;
I'm no cooing turtle dove;
  Treat me rough, kid; treat me rough!

Can the soft and weepy sighs,
  Chop the meek and humble pose.
I'm no cut-glass raffle prize,
  I'm no fragile little rose!
Grab me with a python grip.
  If I struggle, call the bluff.
Want my love? Then take the tip,
  Treat me rough, kid; treat me rough!

I don't want my hand caressed
  With a nice respectful peck;
Yank me wildly to your chest;
  If I fight you, break my neck.
Please don't be a gentle dub,
  Spilling la-de-dah-ish guff,
Woo and win me with a club.
  Treat me rough, kid; treat me rough!

THE LASTING LOOK

When a pretty girl goes by
There's a glimmer in my eye,
Just a flicker of delight
At so glad and fair a sight;
Youth and beauty and romance
These are what my roving glance
Find in every curve and curl
Of a passing pretty girl,
And my heart is beating high
When a lovely maid goes by.

If I yield me to her charm
As she passes, where's the harm?
I'll not follow her, or speak
Words to flush that peach-blow cheek,
But my much-adoring gaze
Dwells upon her as she sways
Daintily a-down the street
Gay and very blithe and sweet.
Love of beauty's not amiss;
Who shall censure me for this?

If I ever get so I
Care not as the girls go by,
If no glance of mine shall rest
On the very prettiest—
Take me quickly then, I pray,
And just bury me away,
For, though I may breathe and move,
My indifference will prove
That the life has gone from me
And I'm dead as dead can be.

TONIC

I'm the mother of three, and I'm Thirty,
 And a Good Little Wife in the home,
And I've never been known to be flirty
 When out on the highways I roam;
But, nevertheless, I must add, I
 Find life is a trifle more sweet
When the men-folks still give me the glad eye
 As I pass on my way down the street.

If I were addressed or molested
 I know how enraged I would be.
I'd have the offender arrested
 For making advances to me.
But, though I'd be terribly mad, I
 Would know I was not quite passé,
Since *Somebody* gave me the glad eye
 And made me feel peppy and gay!

I think that the mashers are awful
 —A nuisance beyond any doubt—
It should be entirely unlawful
 For creatures like that to be out;
But when with a weary and sad eye
 I gaze in the mirror, forsooth,
And then a man gives me the glad eye,
 I feel I've recovered my Youth!

When, worn with devotion to duty
 And feeling a hundred or more,
I hear a man say, "Oh, you Cutie,"
 Of course it's a thing I deplore;
But I do not exactly feel bad, I
 Remark to myself, "Well, you bet
While *Somebody* gives me the glad eye
 There's life in the old lady yet!"

THE RECIPE

Love is made of tenderness, love is made of fire,
Of glory and of wonder and of longing and desire,
Of dreams and hopes and fantasies, of passion and of pain,
Of showers after sunshine and of sunshine after rain.

But love that lasts a lifetime is of more material stuff,
It's made of dogged patience when the going's rather rough,
It's made of understanding of a lot of little things,
The irks and quirks and jolts and jerks that daily living brings.

Love that lasts a lifetime has a sense of humor, too,
Which only grins at silly things that wives and husbands do;
Which bears with dreariness at times and boredom now and
        then,
When sweethearts prove but women and when lovers prove but
        men.

Love that lasts a lifetime learns to struggle and be brave,
To throw a bluff at destiny and make Dame Fate behave,
To take the hard luck with the good, the bitter with the sweet,
And figure rent and clothing bills and what it costs to eat.

Love that lasts a lifetime must be practical—as such
It nags and carps a little, but it shouldn't do it much.
A wifely tear, a manly growl will now and then correct
Some faults and peccadilloes that no patience will affect.

Love that lasts a lifetime needn't lose its high romance,
But it's got to be of fiber that can battle Circumstance,
It must have fire and tenderness, and loyalty intense,
And faith and hope and charity—and Simple Common Sense.

NO RULE TO BE AFRAID OF

The grammar has a rule absurd
    Which I would call an outworn myth;
"A preposition is a word
    You mustn't end a sentence with!"

That rule I very often flout
    Because it makes me far from calm.
It's one I do not care about.
    I wonder where they get it from?

I'll make a preposition do
    The thing I want to use it for.
Why should that be objected to?
    There's nothing in it to abhor.

For since my school days first commenced
    It is a practice which I've found
No reason to protest against
    Amid the folks I've been around.

And though to purists it's a sin
    And one that's largely frowned upon,
It's one that I've persisted in
    Whatever spot I'm dwelling on.

For if to any sentence pat,
    A preposition adds more pith,
And aids what I am driving at
    Why, that is what I'll end it with!

SPACE

There once was a tiny electron
    Who gazed all about him and cried,
"What an infinite thing is an atom,
    How deep and how long and how wide!
Can the mind conceive anything huger?
    Well, I can't, for one, and I've tried!"

An atom peered vaguely around him
    And with every glance that he cast
He thought, "Oh, a molecule's limits
    Are most unbelievably vast.
For cosmic bewildering greatness
    A molecule can't be surpassed!"

Yet the scientist's lens microscopic
    For all of its strength, failed to show
A glimpse of electron or atom
    Or molecule either! And so
We learn a most excellent moral
    Though just what it is I don't know.

. . . I wonder who remembers the greatest World Series copy ever written . . . the series of running stories in verse— fifteen hundred words of it, including four and five changes of pace—all technically correct and describing the games with expert appreciation and delivered each night for the deadline by Berton Braley in 1915.

Westbrook Pegler, New York *World-Telegram*, September 30, 1936

THE MAIN EVENT

Silence! All rumbles of war multifarious,
Silence! The rumor of times most precarious.
Hush all the clamor of politics furious,
Charges and scandals and schemes that are curious;
Cease all the talk of that Greaser imbroglio
Which has been filling each newspaper folio.
Sulzer and Thaw, for the time, cease to worry us.
Tariff and currency simply can't flurry us.
Fandom is tense—and our dignity's gone again.
Brethren, the mighty World Series is on again!

Many a time has this ballad been sung to you.
This is "old stuff" which is cheerfully flung to you.
Still, I refuse to make any apology
When I am warbling of baseball psychology.
Seasons may change, and the rules may be altering,
But the good old grip of the game is unfaltering.
Still the old agony, fever and chill to it,
Still the old rapturous wonder and thrill to it,
Still the old coaching-box chatter and "con" again,
Still the old cheers—for the Series is on again!

"Hey, have they started? Say, what are the batteries?"
"Mathewson's losing his whip—so the chatter is!"
"Don't you believe it; the Big Six is right again,
Chuck full of brains and of vigor and fight again."
"Mebbe so, mebbe so; still I am cynical—"
"Bet you that Baker falls off of his pinnacle—"
"Hi there, you robber; that wasn't a strike at all!"
Same old excitement and, gee, how we like it all!

Boyhood is back, and our years they are gone again,
Brethren, the mighty World Series is on again!

CHANT ROYAL OF WAR

With lances raised the troopers thunder by
   And in the sun their polished helmets flare;
A mass of surging color fills the eye,
   The pennons dip, the brazen trumpets blare;
The infantry, in marching row on row,
Comes swinging past, a brave and sightly show,
   And in the wake of all this massed array
   The grim, forbidding field guns lurch and sway;
The echo of the cheers resounds afar,
   And fools look on this pageantry and say,
"Behold the glory and the pomp of War!"

Thus Emperors and Kings and rulers high
   Send forth their nations' Youth to do and dare;
And how shall humble soldiers question Why?
   The War Lords call, and War is their affair.
Let lovers kiss and cling before they go,
For what the future holds no man may know.
   The children wail, the wives and mothers pray,
   Fearful of all the menace of the fray,
Of lives and loves that war will wreck or mar;
   Only as tawdry shams and lies do they
Behold the glory and the pomp of War!

About deserted fields the blackbirds fly,
   The grain is rotting and the barns are bare,
The shops are empty and the winepress dry,
   The mills are silent, and the furnace glare
Has died to ashes. Creakingly and slow
The ships sway at their hawsers to and fro,
   Denied the salty deeps and flying spray;
   The clutch of famine tightens day by day,
Disease comes stalking where the helpless are
   (Starving and gaunt, with faces pinched and gray)—
Behold the glory and the pomp of War!

Houses and palaces and churches lie
In ruins beyond mending or repair;
War tramples on, though Art and Beauty die
Under his feet that crush, his hands that tear;
The horror and the desolation grow;
War's track is black as if a molten flow
Of seething lava followed on his way.
The beast in Man breaks every bond and stay
And gorges foully without let or bar.
What minstrel hymns these exploits in his lay?
Behold the glory and the pomp of War!

The thunder of the cannon fills the sky
And shrapnel hurtles shrieking through the air;
Men answer battle cry with battle cry
And fall in windrows with their eyes astare.
Red, red the sun seems, with a hateful glow
That beats upon the shambles down below
And lifts a stench of corpses and decay;
Here is no bright parade, no pageant gay,
But bloodlust ruled by some malevolent star
Which drives men on to slay and slay and slay.
Behold the glory and the pomp of War!

L'ENVOI

Some time, somewhere, my Masters, ye shall pay
For all the Wrath and Evil ye let play
While ye stayed safely, free of wound or scar,
And in the Blackness of the Pit ye may
Behold the glory and the pomp of War!

A FABLE FOR POETS

Once on a time there was a bard
    Who made his tuneful lute to twang,
But found the going rather hard,
    Till one day, growing wise, he sang:
"Perhaps my little lays are bad,
    Perhaps you think I sing them wrong,
But—none of them are very sad
    And none of them are very long!"

Ah, then the people filled his hat
    And danced to all the songs he made;
The minstrel waxed exceeding fat
    And joyfully his lute he played.
The king came by and heard the lad
    Carol his promise to the throng,
"None of my songs are very sad
    And none of them are very long!"

"Oh, wondrous minstrel" quoth the king,
    "Oh, wisest of all bards there be,
Come to the royal court and sing
    Thy deathless lyrics unto me."
And so in silk the bard was clad,
    His verses rang the well-known gong,
For none of them were very sad,
    And none of them were very long!

He sang of love and war and work,
    Of little things that men hold dear,
Gay songs wherein the tear-drops lurk,
    Grave songs with smiles behind the tear;
But all his many lyrics had
    A spirit unafraid and strong,
And—none of them were very sad
    And none of them were very long.

Hear, then, this poet's epitaph;
   "He sang of Hope and not Despair,
Of how a man might bravely laugh
   Through all the woes that he must bear;
He made a dull old world seem glad
   With bits of simple, dauntless song,
For none of them were very sad
   And none of them were very long!"

Excerpts from *Pegasus Pulls a Hack:*
Memoirs of a Modern Minstrel

"Give the Kid a Chance"

[At sixteen,] I had to quit high school and go to work—a factory hand in the plow plant in Madison, at four dollars and a half a week. I was promoted to office boy at six dollars after a month or two, and for two years that was my job.

I wasn't quite eighteen when I came back to high school. I was two years and a half behind the class with which I had entered. Should I take three years to finish my course and thus have time for football, or cut out athletics and do the three years in two? I decided to do the three years in two.

And here, for the first time when it might be regarded as important, I bucked up against the "thou shalt not" of the powers that be. The powers that be, with one exception, said that, football or no football, doing three years—to be accurate, three years and a half—of a four year course in two years was (a) "unprecedented; (b) impossible; (c) *verboten.*" Obstinately I determined that I would: (a) do three and a half years in two; (b) play football as well. I had a job on my hands.

My teeth were worn out from gritting, my neck ached from sticking out my chin and taking socks on it. But, as always in my life, and in most lives, I think, there was one fellow willing "to give the kid a chance."

This was George Link, the geometry instructor, who quietly loosened mortar on the stone wall I was butting against, while I kicked and butted and hammered. With George abetting, I broke through that stone wall. The authorities would let me try—but my standings had to be above average.

I dwell on this situation because it was symptomatic of "how I got that way." Because it was the first real test of an innate and irritating persistence which is probably responsible for nine-tenths of my successes, if not ninety-nine and forty-four one-hundredths per cent, and at the same time responsible for a thousand and one petty rows over nothing, for exasperation among my friends, for the making of a select lot of enemies, and for countless failures that tolerance and diplomacy would have avoided.

But it won *this* fight for me. I did the course in two years. I played football. I did my own cooking while my mother was away supporting me. And I decided to be an author.

I decided to be an author because Horatio Winslow, now a well known short story writer and novelist, wrote a parody of the "Stag at Eve," and it appeared in the *Cardinal,* the University paper. Horatio was still in high school, but his parody was given a front page spread. I was proud of Horatio—but if the big stiff could get away with that, so could I.

So I began to write verse. Unlike Horatio's it was abysmally bad verse. I've been poring over some old blank books in which I copied a lot of it, and if anybody today sent me such stuff as the work of a seventeen-year-old lad, my first impulse would be to say there was no hope for his ever writing even saleable verse. But my sounder second thought would be to note only this—had the verses rhythm? Because, given a feeling for rhythm, all other qualities necessary for producing reasonably *acceptable* verse (I am not talking of poetry) can be *learned* and *taught.*

If you can dance, you can, if you want to hard enough, learn to write verse. But if you don't *feel* in your fibers the difference in beat between a fox trot and a one step—stick to prose. And make more money....

It was Horatio Winslow who discovered Tom Hood's "Rhymester" and told me about it. And to Tom Hood (son of Thomas) and his "Rhymester," I owe all that I am professionally, such as it is. For in that little manual I found verse treated not as an inspired art, but as a practical craft—as carpentry with words.

It brushed aside all the bunk about "poetic license" and pointed out that when the "great ones" rhymed "river" and "ever," for an example, the great ones had cheated—and that the young versifier wouldn't become a great one by copying genius in its slipshod moments. Tom Hood told me, when I was eighteen, that there was no such thing as an "allowable rhyme." That two words either rhymed or they didn't.

Tom Hood instructed me that the rhyme is on the accented syllable, and that therefore you can't rhyme "trouble" with "sell," or "bluebird" with "word," but must rhyme "trouble" with "double" or "rubble" or "bubble," and "bluebird" with some arrangement like "true bird" or "glue bird." Tom Hood also averred that rhymes must begin with a different consonant sound, and that while "agree" and "decree" were rhymes, "agree" and "degree" were not rhymes but identities. And that though the French poets, from Villon down, had entered into a gentleman's agreement that "*fait*" and "*parfait*"—for an illustration—were rhymes, that didn't make them so either in English, French or Chaldean. After thirty years of practicing verse and discussing it, I have yet to find any valid argument to shake any of these Hoodian dicta. Rhyme is rhyme and nothing else is rhyme but rhyme, and when either great or minor bards give you assonance or approximation in place of it, their lines are flawed in that particular. I am not arguing with you, I am telling you.

Tom Hood further opined—and I am opining the same to this day—that verse should be written as nearly like prose as possible. Not like prose in its choice of words or its color and sentiment, but like prose in its mechanical arrangement of language and thought.

Tom frowned on inversions. He objected to tortuous constructions obviously done for the sake of rhyme. Tom held that a good versifier could avoid these twistings and topsy-turvyings if he worked at the job hard enough. Tom was right—the best versifiers and poets can and do.

Tom averred that there was seldom need, if a versifier knew his meters, to sprinkle "o'ers" and "e'ers" and "'neaths" and "in'ts," "e'ens" and "'wares" among his lines. He didn't like, and regarded as pretentious and unnecessary, such words as "athwart," "bemused," "forespent," and other archaic or pompous expressions that were no longer part of simple, natural speech.

He said the versifiers' rhymes should ring clear and true, but should not chime in pairs that had been worn thin by much usage—that the versifier should strive for freshness and novelty without sacrificing clarity and ease.

Tom was a strict disciplinarian—but, in my opinion, a golden master. And a course under him today would brush out of a lot of lofty brows a mess of twaddle and bunk about poetry. I don't know of a rule he states, or of an axiom he sets down, that isn't a standard by which not only light verse but the greatest of epics can be simply and accurately judged. And when I violate his rules, as I do frequently, I never kid myself that it's for the sake of the "higher art" which is above the restrictions of a mere text on versification. I violate his rules because I'm lazy, or hurried or slovenly, and my verse fails of excellence to exactly the degree I depart from his sane and wise dicta.

Examine the work of any poet or "mere versifier" you please, using the kind of plain horse sense you use in judging any other work of man, and you'll find his wanderings from the fundamental rules of prosody are evils and not virtues of his style.

On such a solid base of unyielding fundamentals, Tom Hood bade the apprentice erect the structure of rhyme. And then he gave the beginner the rules of scansion so that his walls might be straight and his floors level. Further he supplied blue prints of expert architecture in verse. In other words, he gave samples and quotations of the types of meter, and the forms of verse used by great craftsmen. Here, in Tom Hood, I first learned definitely—with tangible models—what constituted a couplet, triplet, quatrain, quintet and octette. From there I could move on to sonnets, triolets, rondeaux, rondels, ballades, double ballades, pantoums, chant royals, and sestinas. Each demonstrated by masters of the particular form.

Here was something definite, tangible and solid to work with. Here were working models and tools with which to "build your own." Keats, opening Chapman's "Homer," couldn't have known a more heartshaking thrill than I found in this modest little volume.

I risked the success of my "two year plan" by spending many a study hour in trying to fit my adolescent ideas within the strait walls of sonnets and ballades. I sat up to all hours fashioning triolets and rondeaux in imitation of the models from Dobson and Lang and Henley furnished by Tom Hood. I spent literal days in the public library reading the deft meters of Guy Wetmore Carryl, of Swinburne, Calverley, Locker-Lampson, Thomas Hood, Praed, Frank Dempster Sherman, Clinton Scollard—and any other poet whose technical dexterity was particularly adept. These are mostly minors? Absolutely, Mr. Shean. I was trying to teach my Percheron-footed Pegasus to prance like a racer, and the practitioners of light verse would show me how to do that far better than the earth-shaking masters. I was trying to learn versification—ease and adaptability and skill in handling rhyme, and I very wisely, I think, imitated those whose work was distinguished chiefly by "manner." When I had learned "manner," I thought, "matter" would take care of itself. If I had the stuff, I was more likely to write poetry by first learning to write verse; and if I didn't have the stuff, a sufficiently facile handling of rhymes and meters might serve to make me an entertaining poetaster, anyhow.

Thus from both the poetic and the purely practical viewpoint, I believe my concentration on form and technique was sound. I believe it is sound for anybody, poet or jingler, to learn to be a good carpenter before he tries to be a master builder. I cannot, for the life of me, see anything magnificent in free versifiers who scorn the limitations they are too lazy to learn, and "express themselves" untrammeled by rhyme, reason, ratiocination or rule. Everybody knows that a pianist must learn finger exercises before he plays rhapsodies, and that an engineer has to learn drafting before he builds skyscrapers, but to regard poetry as a craft to be learned before it's an art to be practiced seems to strike many critics as an attitude of dull unfeeling philistinism.

The fact is, and it can be demonstrated to the satisfaction of anybody but the pontifical poetry theorists, that the greatest poets are the greatest technicians, and that where they sag—as all but Keats do sag in places—it is in moments where their technique and not their thought, fail them.

Do I seem to contradict myself? If the greatest poets are the greatest technicians, why did I study the minors first?

No, I don't contradict myself. I studied the minors first because they use, for their purposes of light verse, a more complicated *mechanical* dexterity than is usual in serious poetry. Half the fun of light verse *is* its pure virtuosity. If I could practice on that, if I could get to handle fixed French forms, toss off double and triple rhymes with moderate ease, I might gain a suppleness and grace that certainly wouldn't desert me when I essayed more classic measures. Besides, it was the idea of doing light verse that chiefly attracted me. I thought it was an art—I think so now—but chiefly I thought it was a craft I'd like to learn and that I might conceivably practice with success. I didn't think of myself as a poet, but as somebody who *might* become a versifier. I don't think of myself as a poet now (in which opinion many people concur) but—I did become a versifier. And a good one, if I do say it myself. And I became a good versifier because at eighteen I found Tom Hood's "Rhymester," tried to write every form of verse he presented, imitated every poet he mentioned and a number I discovered for myself, and kept on imitating all of them until I evolved what I suppose is my own style.

As I recall, it was when I was deepest in the intricacies of sestinas and chants royal and Tom Hood, that I announced to my mother my definite decision to be a writer. There was nothing to justify my ambition except that one verse sold to *Judge*; there was very little in the other verse I was doing to make anybody believe I'd ever sell much, but I'd made up my mind I'd be a writer and, consciously or subconsciously, I held to that doggedly through nearly eight years before I could make it a fact. Just that nagging, irritating, unremitting persistence which I must have been born with, my main asset and my greatest liability.

"The World Was Nothing To Be Afraid Of"

[At the end of a summer spent (unsuccessfully) selling books, during Braley's college years, he set off homeward from Buffalo via boat:]

The skipper did put me to work—in the coal hole—but later he relented and made me a sort of cabin boy, so that was all right and I slipped off the boat in Milwaukee, hopped the blind of a train for Madison, and thus got home, broke, filthy and somehow more confident of myself in a big world.

Well, why not? I had sold enough books to keep from wholly starving, I had seen cities and men—slums unimaginable and splendors marvelous; I had learned enough book agent technique to be useful to me later on when I attacked New York editors in their dens; I had been the guest of greatness and in love with loveliness; and, finally, I had beaten my way for most of the distance home by boat and train! Huh—the world was nothing to be afraid of.

Nor is it; the realists, the futilists, the fatalists, the whinists, the whimperists, the ironists and the gloomists to the contrary notwithstanding. It isn't the "best of all possible worlds," but it's the best world with which I happen to be acquainted. And on the whole, it's been about as good to me as I fancy I deserve. And even if the sentient or insentient forces that rule it had given *me* a rotten deal, I would hesitate to declare that it was all wrong because it had been wrong to me. Somehow the wailers and gnashers of teeth about the "crool, crool world" seem to me to be complaining because the regiment is out of step with them and is continually treading on their sore heels.

I am a realist to the extent that I recognize, and do my little best to combat and to remedy, the stupidities, the injustices, the cruelties and the clumsy inefficiencies of life as a good reporter must see them. But I am an idealist and a romanticist in believing that it is not a malign and ineluctable fate that decrees life *must* be so, nor that fumbling, stumbling and groping humanity is doomed by its natural depravity always to feel its way in semi-darkness.

(If this seems to collide with my simile about being out of step with the regiment—let it collide.)

I am Pollyanna enough to think that that same dumb and myopic mankind is fumbling a little more effectively toward betterment as it moves with time, that civilization is gradually fitting humanity's near-sighted eyes with more skillfully ground lenses, and that we get a little clearer vision—and use what we have more wisely—as we, the world, get older. And those other sentimental and mawkish Pollyannas, those "glad boys" who write history, not in dates and battles, but in terms of folks and how they lived—and live, support my philosophy.

Compared with an ideal world, this one is a mess—even if your ideal and mine don't resemble each other in the least. But stacked up against either the Dark or the Golden Ages of the remote or the proximate past (see any *factual* history) it doesn't look so hopeless.

And I'm such an incurable and incorrigible romanticist as to tingle and thrill in my senile and decrepit fibers more than I did in my youth, over the congenital, indomitable, zestful, resurgent and gallantly courageous spirit of Man. Attaboy, *hominidae*—you're *there!*

A world in which such spirit is predominant—and don't sniffle that it isn't—is not a world to be afraid of. I've registered timidity and trepidation before it many's the time, but being scared of a horse doesn't prove he's dangerous. It just shows you don't know how to judge horses. And honestly, and at the risk of being snubbed as a complacent old platitudinist, I have to reiterate that the world has been as kind, as decent, as fair to me as my nature and my few talents warranted. I shall doubtless—as I have already—discuss subjectively many situations and conditions in which I personally have received an apparently unprovoked sock on the jaw from fate. I shall relate and review much tough sledding and bumpy riding on corduroy roads. But, viewed objectively, I am inclined to think I got the jolts on the jaw because I hadn't learned to box well enough, and that much, if not all, of the tough sledding and rough riding was due to taking the wrong roads. I've *got* to believe that not *all* my hard luck was my own fault, because if I didn't, I'd lose what self-confidence I still retain—but if I dared to be completely scientific in my self-analysis, I'm afraid I would find my troubles should be signed "by Berton Braley."

So it seems to my doddering intellect that the consistent apostle of futility can be true to his philosophy only by committing suicide.

That if he remains in life at all, he is admitting that there is some hope—if only the hope of writing about hopelessness. And that to take the world as you find it, to do your small best to better it, to get as much fun as you can out of it, is not only a sound theory of life—but is, consciously or unconsciously, the actual practice of optimists and pessimists alike.

If I could live up to this, my theory of life, I'd be a grand guy. Anyhow, I have the fun of *thinking* what a grand guy I'd be if I lived up to it.

Once in a while I have come near it, at least so far as my personal difficulties were concerned. There was the matter of my thesis for senior year. A thesis is an essay you have to write to graduate. It is supposed to represent the cream of all the knowledge you've gained from the studies in which you've majored. And therefore you are supposed to be working on it during the entire senior year. Nobody but a grind *does* work on it until a month or two before graduation, and the faculty knows that, but isn't supposed to.

My original idea for a thesis didn't work out. Whereupon I went to the head of my department, Professor W. A. Scott, and requested permission to write another thesis. I had plenty of time—Professor Scott knew perfectly well that I had time, but:

"Impossible!" he snapped.

I had never loved Professor Scott; I do not love him now. It does not seem to me that a true educator would discourage youth from attempting even the impossible—purely for reasons of academic routine. Nor that a liberal-minded pedagogue would follow that youth from the office of one professor to another, tripping his feet and hamstringing his knees, as the youth made his pilgrimage in search of a proctor who would allow him to try a new thesis.

But I persistently limped on until I reached Professor Reinsch . . . who was unfettered by academic cannots, unawed by scholastic shalt nots, and unprejudiced by Professor Scott's disciplinary dicta.

Like George Link in high school, he said, "Give the kid a chance," and gave it to me. I lived in the University Library for that final month, I let all my other studies slide, I read and really digested nearly fifty books—for my thesis required wide reading, and finally, calling upon all the concentration cramming for exams had taught me, I wrote that twenty-thousand-word thesis in approximately twenty hours of continuous effort—and got under the wire in time to qualify.

And so the "noble youth" graduated. Well, I think I *was* rather a noble youth to beat that rap from life! My B.A. meant nothing to me as a degree but it meant everything to me as evidence that I had definitely completed the job of going through college. That I had finished what I started.

It's no world to be afraid of, for there is always a Professor Reinsch to overbalance the Professor Scott—and if you don't find your Professor Reinsch when you need him, blame yourself, not the world. For he's always available, if you search far enough.

I was through with college and free to survey the world I'd decided not to fear. The manner of conducting this survey had been all worked out. I would get two or three large newspapers and a magazine or so to commission me as a roving correspondent and I would go places and do things. . . .

Jerre Murphy, once secretary to Senator La Follette, and (in 1905) editor of the *Butte Inter-Mountain*, was one of those to whom I had sent my circular letter regarding possibilities of casual correspondence. Murphy wired me:

"NOT INTERESTED IN CORRESPONDENCE BUT IF YOU WANT JOB AS NEWSPAPER MAN OFFER YOU TWENTY A WEEK AS APPRENTICE REPORTER. WIRE IF ACCEPTABLE AND I WILL FORWARD TRANSPORTATION."

"Round the World as a Tramp Royal"* was a great and glamorous idea—but *twenty dollars a week* was important money to a young college grad in those days. And Butte was West—and on the way 'round. . . .

Newspaperman in Butte:
"For the First Time I Stood on My Own"

Butte! There was a town!

Bleak, gaunt and ugly to the unaffectionate eye; a camp on a scarred and barren hill, surrounded by more barren hills and nearly desolate flats that stretched away to bald and ragged peaks, Butte came in an astonishingly short time to look beautiful to me.

In "Shoestring," the novel I wrote in 1929, the description of "Maverick" was my memory of Butte.

"It is easy to gird at the 'wide open spaces where men are men' but when Scotland and Cornwall and Finland and Scandinavia, to say

*Author's Note: This being the autobiography of a versifier, all quotations not otherwise designated are from the auto-biographer's personal files.

nothing of New England, Texas, California and the middle west, seemed to have bred their biggest males for the job of mining copper in Maverick, the men-ness of men in this rugged town of the wide open spaces is just one of the many facts of life that the intelligentsia don't know.

"In that lusty gang of thick-thewed giants the ordinary six-footer was a runt. Height and bulk and he-ness ruled in office, shop and trade. Men who were men in the open spaces, men who would be men in the crowdedest places. And men who lived high, wide and handsome in a wide open town."

"For though frame shacks had been succeeded by brick cottages or mansions, and false front wooden stores by six, eight and ten story office structures, twenty-four years ago Maverick was still in essence a roistering, swaggering pioneer mining camp, with few of its best families even one generation removed from sweating in hot stopes or serving, behind bar or gaming table, those who did.

"Bars that had opened twenty years before hadn't used or needed a key since. Still, at the Colorado and the Nevada and the Montana, you could toss your wad on the whirr of the wheel, risk it on the next card in the faro deck, or shoot it on the ivories that tumbled merrily over the green cloth.

"An ugly town, a raw town, a hard-fighting, hard-living, hard-drinking town, but also a gay, gallant, careless and tonic town."

So I described "Maverick" and such was Butte. Only that you ceased soon to be aware of its ugliness and instead found a certain strange loveliness in its raw colors and rough contours. Slag heaps and ore dumps, weathered with wind and rain and sun into heaps of pigment—sienna, flame, jade, crimson, turquoise, and hot gold. Mine hoists metamorphosed into tall spires of industry, delicate against the bright blue sky. Trestles and even smelter chimneys changed into cubistic designs that somehow fitted into the terrain and its mighty activities. . . .

When I arrived there, the few remaining smelters occasionally filled the otherwise bracing and tangy air with a white fog of sulphur smoke, and street cars sometimes felt their way through it with bells clanging, and you brushed aside a cloud of it in order to see the waiter to whom you were giving your breakfast order, and everybody coughed and cursed; but after all, it fumigated the town, and there wasn't any infectious disease, and most of us were young and healthy, so what the heck! . . .

. . . Butte—where for the first time I stood wholly on my own feet, where for the first time I learned what it was to judge men and women by *what* they were and not *who* they were, and to be similarly judged myself; where for the first time it was actually up to me to make good without influence or background and find out what real stuff I had for getting along with a world that made no allowances for me. It was grand—and after I got used to it, it was more fun than any of those dear college days had ever afforded. . . .

Horatio Alger's heroes had nothing on me for ambition and industry. I undertook my assignments, to chronicle hotel arrivals and to note garnishee actions in justice court as diligently as though they were major murder cases. And I applied my young imagination and invention to giving as much color and as much news value to these petty stories as I knew how. And with all my eagerness, enthusiasm and application, I searched the streets, alleys, nooks and crannies of Butte—as they became more familiar—for items that would fatten my string and demonstrate my efficiency.

I volunteered also to write a verse a day, my reward to be merely a "by" line. And I wrote little feature stories out of personals, and tossed off purely creative tales and skits that I thought might please a reader or two and acquire me merit with those who paid my salary.

But something went haywire with the Horatio Alger recipe. Instead of bigger and better assignments, I had taken away from me even those I had. Whenever I happened on a *real* story in a justice court, hotel or business office, some other reporter was sent to develop my tip. What the Horatio Alger system hadn't allowed for was the fact that the city editor didn't like me. He was a soft-voiced, sweet-mannered, apparently considerate person who revealed no animus whatsoever, but who killed my stories, curtailed my chances, reduced my assignments, used me as a copy boy instead of a reporter—and then pointed out to Jerre Murphy my diminishing share in producing the stuff that filled the *Inter-Mountain*'s columns.

With the results that after my first year (you will note that my pause in Butte on my world tramp was already longer than I anticipated) Jerre Murphy called me into his office and told me I was a losing proposition.

"I thought you'd make a newspaper man," he said, "but I guess I was mistaken. However, perhaps it's because you're spending so much time trying to write for magazines."

"It's my own time, Mr. Murphy," I said. "If I'd rather work than play in my evenings, that seems to me my concern."

"It seems to me mine," replied my boss. "If you'll cut it out I'll keep you on and give you another chance. Oh, yes, and you'll have to quit fooling with those jingles. They're not worth ten cents a week to this paper."

. . . I was broke and in debt. But the price of keeping my job was too high.

"I quit," I said.

One block down the street was the *Evening News* office. I went to see Dick Kilroy.

"Can you use a cub reporter?" I said. "I've just quit the *Inter-Mountain*."

"No," replied Kilroy.

"That's tough for me," I said, and turned to go.

Kilroy grinned.

"I don't think you're a cub," he said. "I've read some of your signed stuff in the *Inter-Mountain*. Why did you quit?"

"To keep from being fired—they don't think I'm much good."

"What do you think?"

"I don't think they gave me much chance to be good, but I may be mistaken."

"I need a man for police," he said. "Will twenty-seven fifty be o.k.? You'll have to work like hell for it."

"You've hired a man," I said. "Oh, but wait. I had another reason for quitting. Murphy objected to my writing for magazines,—or trying to."

"On office time?"

"On my own, in the evenings."

"What the hell business was that of his? Come in Monday."

And—here the Horatio Alger formula began to function again—on Monday I scored four sizable news beats over the *Inter-Mountain*! I can taste that triumph now. Not a reporter? Heh! heh!

You see, again somebody came along in time to "give the kid a break."

This man Kilroy had what the movies now seek so assiduously to find or build—glamor. I know a few of the great, many of the near-great, and flocks of personalities. Put Dick Kilroy at table with any of them and they glitter mostly in his radiance. A temperamental, volatile, unpredictable Irishman, with a silver tongue and a golden humor. . . .

Working for him was to live on intellectual cocktails, compounded of a pony of enthusiasm, a pony of insanity, a pony of inspiration, large measures of indefatigable industry, jiggers of bitterness and exasperation, and dashes of a dozen other ingredients such as intuition, vacillation, whimsy, delirium tremens and brass knuckles. The recipe for a Kilroy cocktail was never twice the same.

He was the most unreasonable, unfair and intolerant tyrant I've ever known, and the most amenable, just and liberal boss. If Cooney, Mackintosh, O'Malley and I, who constituted the city staff, got beat on *one* story, he would stage an act of passion and tragedy that Edwin Booth never bettered, threaten to fire us all—and maybe fire one or two of us—; cool down fifteen minutes later, forget he'd fired anybody, buy everybody a drink, and tell the world he had the liveliest, loyalist, smartest staff in the Northwest. He was immaculate in his dress, and his office was knee-deep in disorder. He was lazy—and could accomplish more in half an hour than most men can do in a day. He piled more work on our shoulders than we could possibly do—and we did it. Partly because he paid us better than any other staff in town, but chiefly because there was something magic in him that stimulated and inspired effort. He believed responsibility develops men, and in this belief he had no hesitancy in putting the greenest reporter on the biggest assignment.

"He'll be so nervous," said Dick, "that he'll work twice as hard on it as a star. What if he doesn't write as good a story—that can be fixed in the office, and if the kid's any good, I find it out early. This long apprenticeship on hotel arrivals and so forth is a lot of poppycock."

Well, he followed out that theory. Within a month of my joining the *News*, Kilroy had had me on police, labor, politics and courts, had given me a chance to write editorials, put me in charge of the sport page while Mackintosh covered police for me, and, in fact, used me in every department of the news end of the paper except office boy. Kilroy wasn't that kind of a boss—he might make a reporter out of an office boy, but never an office boy out of a reporter.

So for three jittery but joyous years—save six months' exile in Billings when the mines shut down, and six weeks in the mines when our pressmen went on strike—I was a reporter for the *Butte Evening News*, under Richard R. Kilroy.

If I seem to allot this man Kilroy disproportionate space in these memoirs, it is only seeming! The man who gives you your first real chance, who boosts and badgers and jolts and jabs you on your upward way, who tells you you're good when he thinks you are, and sometimes tells you you're rotten when you're not so hot, whose intelligence, perception and imagination are as quick and sensitive as you're ever going to encounter, who pays you well and demands your best, and who backs you against any and all outside powers you butt up against in doing your job for him—

That man *can't* occupy disproportionate space in your memoirs. . . .

When I read of the terrific pressure of New York journalism, I am "leffink." By comparison with the amount of work we did on the *News,* and the pace of it, reporting on a New York "madhouse sheet" is a gentle drift down the stream of time. . . . *We,* with four men on the street, were competing with city rooms employing eight, ten and fifteen reporters.

Thus my training in newspaper work was a combination of the small-town idea of all inclusive news-gathering, with the big city emphasis on color, feature, human interest and reportorial skill in handling news. It meant necessary industry in getting stories and efficiency in presenting them. We had no copywriters—and we wrote our own heads. And since Kilroy jumped with both feet on any story and any head that was vapid and drab, I learned to put pep in both— which, in the case of head lines, is somewhat of an art, for column rules are tighter than the laws of Medes and Persians. Kilroy had another conviction—that no news story was worth more than five hundred words. It is a conviction I still share, with the wise allowances you have to make now and then.

To keep the thought of brevity before us, Dick supplied us with copy paper on which, even single-spaced, you couldn't crowd more than five hundred words. The result was a paper which, for succinctness, simplicity and interest in the presentation of news I have yet to see excelled. "Breakovers" were confined almost entirely to telegraph stories—local stuff ended, and quickly, on the page where it started.

. . . Kilroy's madhouse was no asylum for the slow, the lazy or the unwilling.

I didn't print much verse in the *News,* because I hadn't much time. However, though I didn't give any particular thought to it, this job of mine was doing more for my writing career than all the verse and prose I had written for the *Inter-Mountain,* or that I was now sending out on the merry-go-round of Uncle Sam's mail.

For in Kilroy's madhouse I was learning to:

> Write whether I felt like it or not.
> Write without any regard to conversations at my elbow or noises and distractions of any other sort.
> Write the thing as I saw it so that other people might see it.
> Write the right word in the right place without fumbling.
> Write simply, clearly and briefly.
> Write to measure—adapt the expression of my ideas to the space and time at my disposal.

And if any critic says this last is prostitution or subversion of art or something, he simply doesn't know anything about the writing craft.

I don't want the gentle reader to believe that I believe I do all these things in my work, now. I know perfectly well that all I do is occasionally to approximate such performance. But these six factors in the production of newspaper copy are also the six most important factors in the *production* of the author's work. Imagination, inspiration, intelligence, talent, genius, whatever you care to call them are only the writer's original equipment. It is these other six factors that make that mental machinery operate to produce literature—(slang for what gets printed).

Put in words, these six factors are, again:

> Industry
> Concentration
> Insight
> Exactness
> Simplicity
> Adaptability

If some of my earlier remarks appear to belittle industry, I must clarify. Of course industry is essential—I was only objecting to the glorification of a necessity as a virtue.

(1) *Industry.*

I loaf often when I don't feel like working. But thanks to Kilroy's madhouse, I know I am generally coddling myself on these occasions, and that I *could* work if I would. And that healthy feeling of guilt keeps me from coddling myself indefinitely.

(2) *Concentration.*

Not all writers have this particular type. Perhaps it isn't necessary. But it does enable one to do his work with or without a particular sound proof room or without sending the family out for the afternoon; and in almost any circumstances—which is convenient, and saves fuss.

(3) *Insight.*

Maybe this should be put down as part of the natural equipment of a writer, but what I have, I got from reporting what I saw and putting it down on copy paper.

(4) *Exactness.*

Fitting the right word in the right place is a hard job. But it's easier if you've been compelled by the pressure of time in a newspaper office to pick it swiftly out of your mind with a fairly deft hand—as a skilled compositor takes type from a font—instead of fumbling for it with an amateur's fingers.

(5) *Simplicity.*

Why discuss that one?

(6) *Adaptability.*

All I can say is that if a writer can't adapt his style and his matter to the unities of time and space and people—he isn't, in my opinion, a writer. As Quiller-Couch told his students at Cambridge:

"There are two facets to writing, expression and impression, of which impression is far the more important. If you can't impress what you have to express in terms that the world will understand, you have fallen down flat on your job."

Well, anyhow, these are axioms to me, and if I didn't actually learn all of them in the *Butte Evening News* office, it was there that they became the animating forces in my work. I again protest that I am not always, and perhaps not often, industrious, concentrated, perceptive, exact, simple or adaptable, but I know that what success I have is measured by my approximation to these standards.

"Art Belongs in the Marketplace"

Just once did Kilroy's and my ideas of mutual loyalty clash. The collision came over a comparatively trivial news item.

Heinze* wanted to run a spur track down one of Butte's outlying streets.

"Braley," said Kilroy, "write about three sticks in favor of building that spur."

I endeavored to dodge. "I'm all tied up on other stuff, Dick. Ask Cooney, won't you?"

"I'm asking *you.*"

"Well, if Cooney's busy, why not O'Malley?"

"What's the idea? Have you got paralyzed fingers?"

"Well, if you must know, Dick, it's a matter of principle with me. I don't believe in running railroad tracks down public streets, however unfrequented."

"Well, well, what a public conscience our Berton has suddenly acquired! Now just suppose as your boss I *order* you to write the story, instead of requesting it?"

"Dick," I said, "I like my job. But I can't write that story. I can't write anything that goes against my few civic scruples. It's all right with me to 'lay off' stories, when that's orders, but I can't write in favor of something I oppose, orders or no orders. Maybe that's a fine distinction, but it isn't fine to me. So if I *have* to write that story to hold my job, why—I can't hold my job."

"God!" said Kilroy, "what nobility of purpose. Go to hell!"

Which closed the incident. Cooney wrote the story. The spur was built. Writing the story didn't hurt Cooney's conscience whatever. Not that he hadn't as much conscience as I—only advocating spur tracks for Heinze was no jar to *his* conviction.

But I had stuck by my modest standards of literary probity at the risk of my job. Which was, I think, important. There's always a time one has to meet such a test of convictions, and that was mine. I believe I've held to those standards with reasonable constancy. But, on the other hand, I don't believe in unreasonable standards. . . .

Thus I think that Art Young, for an instance, was admirable, but mistaken, in refusing to work for a great syndicate. Because Art Young is not all socialist and revolutionist. He is also among the world's greatest, gentlest and most charming of humorists. And one of the world's mildest, kindest and most lovable of men.

The syndicate wanted Art chiefly for his humorous work. It would not demand of him any pro-capitalistic cartoons. He was still free to do as much revolutionary stuff as he chose for radical journals.

*Editor's Note: Butte papers were all "organs," controlled by the major mining companies. The *News* was owned by the young maverick copper magnate F. Augustus Heinze, and his friends.

He turned the job down, with the result that his work appeared *only* in the revolutionary press, where it got small circulation—and *that* among people who were already of Art Young's party. It seems to me he accomplished less for his cause than by the more practical course. He denied a vast public the pleasure and stimulation of his work, he lost a chance for wide circulation of at least some of his political ideas, he denied himself the advertising, the influence and power that would automatically have increased his freedom of expression. For the man with a great reputation can take more liberties with his public than one without it. Witness Mr. Shaw, also a socialist.

If Art felt this was "selling his soul," I must admire him for refusing to sell and choosing comparative obscurity to affluence and popularity. But in a world of limitations, I don't think recognizing limitations is selling your soul. It isn't, in my opinion, a matter of conscience, but of commonsense.

I'm arguing this out at length here because, in my writing career, I have been called a "prostitute" by several critics and amateur poets—never by a professional. These judges are everlastingly confusing commercialism with prostitution.

For I'm commercial. Try making a living as a bard any other way! And I have no excuses to offer. I do the type of work my buyers want unless it's something I can't honorably undertake. And whether it's Poetry with a large P or advertising or greeting cards, I do it as well as I can and for as much pay as possible. Raphael, Michelangelo, Shakespeare and Balzac did the same. (I am not rating myself with these gentlemen except in commercial candor.) If these jobs I do are not Art, what of it?

I honestly believe that sound commercialism is the best test of true value in art. People work hard for their money and if they won't part with it for your product the chances are that your product hasn't sufficient value. An artist or writer hasn't any monopoly. He can't say "buy my book" or "purchase my picture"—or "go without books or pictures" as an electric light company, for instance, can say "use our current at our rates—or use candles."

If the public response to his artistry is lacking, he'd do well to spend more time analyzing what's the matter with his work, and less time figuring what's the matter with the public.

That some splendid work has gone commercially unrecognized is perfectly true, but if you like to gamble with the percentage in your favor, bet that the man who sells will, generally speaking, rate the notice of posterity beyond the man who doesn't. . . .

So I don't think working for your living as a writer is prostitution. And I don't think doing odd jobs of writing that "aren't art" is prostitution. Doing these things, in my opinion, doesn't affect my ability to write Art—if anybody can tell me exactly what that means. I think practice and performance of a multiplicity of jobs actually keeps you supple and competent.

Well, if this isn't prostitution of Art, what is?

I'll tell you what I think is prostitution. I think it would have been prostitution for me to have written that story advocating the spur track. Because I'd truly have been selling my convictions for money—for my pay. I think it is prostitution to write anything you *don't* believe. I think it is prostitution deliberately to *write down*—for money. (Incidentally, nobody can do that for long and get away with it.) It is prostitution, in my opinion, to do less than your best with the job you undertake.

If that job is writing an ad or a greeting card, you'll give your best energies to it. If you despise advertising and abominate the product you're publicizing, if you look down on greeting cards, and take the jobs purely because there is money in them, you're a prostitute. And you're a particularly mean and vicious prostitute if you do a second-rate job simply because you think you can get away with it. . . .

That philosophy applies to writers as well as to painters. To my possibly prejudiced eye, the application of Art to commerce is good for commerce and good for Art. I think Art belongs in the market place and not in the cloister. When business began reaching out for first rate artists to design automobile bodies and bathrooms and kitchen cabinets and even egg beaters, beauty and color and line became something we live with instead of something we had to go to museums to find. And the flexibility and power of artistic genius were enhanced rather than lessened by this commercial practice.

Anyhow, as far as I am concerned, this is not apology for practice, but clarification of a writing philosophy. I do advertising because it pays and I wouldn't do it if it didn't pay, but I attempt to sell only those products I am truly "sold on," and then I give that particular job all the skill I possess—as earnestly and honestly as though I were trying to write an epic. I've done greeting cards, mottoes, calendars and bridge scores—in the same spirit. I've written verse for about every type of trade journal there is, sung of machine tools, electric toasters, coal breakers, Mergenthalers, vacuum cleaners, ships and shoes and sealing wax. I did a daily poem for a syndicate for nearly four years. I enjoyed the work, valued the experience, and am proud of what I did with these jobs. The daily poems were not daily master-pieces, but they were the best daily poems in my system. And, in "grinding them out," I hit as high a *percentage* of worthwhile material as I averaged with more leisurely production. . . .

Here's a nice place to answer that question every author is asked to answer every time he meets a non-author. And in my case I have to answer it oftener than most authors, because being a versifier I write more single pieces than a novelist or short story man.

The usual form of the query is, "How do you get your ideas? Do they come to you out of the air or do you go after them?"

The answer is "yes."

I pick up hunches out of the air—from clouds, blue skies, skyscraper towers, winds and the planes that ride them. I also get hunches from the "earth beneath and the waters under the earth." . . .

These are the "inspirational ideas." They make about one-tenth of my product. The other nine-tenths are "perspirational ideas." Those I chase with grim and dogged purpose because it's time to produce—and there ain't no ideas coming "out of the air."

To get ideas this way means intense concentration on a diverse world. I think of forty sources of "copy," dismiss thirty-nine, reduce the thirty-ninth to its constituents and get a subject for verse out of one of them. Or I think of a place to sell verse, and it gives me an idea for a piece that might fit that market, and thus I produce something that I couldn't otherwise have written.

If this sounds sordid—maybe it is. But the fact is that fully as much of my best work has been evolved out of this sordid fashion as has been produced by the divine *afflatus* (hunch) that descends from the stratosphere.

And if a poet, or any writer, tells you these harshly practical methods are not in his philosophy or his work, he is either a liar or an amateur.

Making Pegasus occasionally pull a peddler's wagon may seem pro-fanation to some people, but I think it keeps him from going fat and logy with lack of exercise. If you possess a genuine Pegasus, he'll leap out of the shafts now and then and go bounding over the hills, any-how, and you can't stop him. If your supposed Pegasus is actually a

cart horse, he's more use in the shafts than in the stable. And a ped-
dler's cart, with Pegasus or a plug pushing against the collar takes you
places, brings you close to nature and to humanity, and I am inclined
to think that you see deeper into people's lives when you drive
Pegasus up to their doors and chaffer with them on the porch, than if
you view them from the back of Pegasus in the clouds. Then, too, for
me, every pot and pan, every gadget and device that rattles and bangs
against the sides of the wagon has its own little wonder and magic.
Nor need such quaint radiance as a peddler may find in the common-
place, dazzle his vision so that he cannot see the immense glory of
piled clouds about a setting sun, moonlight mantling the soft curves
of the hills, or morning mist swirling over the waters of a blue lake.

Giddap, Pegasus! Or, if you prefer, Giddap, Napoleon!

"The Romance and Wonder of [the] Commonplace"

Somewhere about 1906, the pressmen went on strike and all four
Butte dailies shut down. On thirty-five dollars a week, I was just as
thriftless as on twenty, so I had no money. But the mines hadn't
shut down, and I went up on the hill and got me a job in the Minnie
Healy...

For the six weeks of the strike, I sweated in hot stopes as a miner.
Since I wasn't looking for "color," but for a living, I was conscious of
getting nothing out of mining but blistered hands, a sore back and
four dollars a day. What I *did* get out of it was the material with which
I was to break into New York three years later. But we never know,
do we? Looking back, I seem to have recognized none of my "breaks"
until several years after they came.

So swift, vivid and exciting were work and play in Butte, so tin-
gling with the zest of the moment, that thought of the long-visioned
literary future of mine was partially relegated to the subconscious
brain. I continued to pound my typewriter industriously on frequent
nights, but with a nagging sense of a duty to a conscientiously main-
tained ambition rather than with inspired purpose. The drama of the
immediate life about me was far more absorbing. . . .

. . . Of course when the *Technical World* bought—actually bought—
for fifteen dollars the "Miracle Workers," I was tremendously elated.
I was more so when they spread it over two pages with illustrations.
It read even better in print—well, your stuff always does, and thank
heaven, I still enjoy a tingle when mine is published.

In the "Miracle Workers," with no definite idea of doing anything but a piece of verse about the kind of roughnecks who were at that time working on the grade of the St. Paul railroad, I had hit on the fundamental idea of the romance and wonder of commonplace and unromantic things and people. It was tuned to the rhythm and beat of a machine age—an age throbbing with more adventure, glamor, magic and romance than Babylon, Troy, Camelot or Carcassonne ever imagined. . . .

The lesson of the "Miracle Workers" hadn't, however, sunk in. I didn't realize that the "Miracle Workers" sold because it was a poem about people and things I *knew*, not a poem about poems, or a poem about things I thought poems should be about, which was characteristic of so much of my earlier stuff.

That writing about life as I saw and knew it was the way to write hit me as an unprecedented idea along in the spring of 1909. It suddenly occurred to me that I could dig poetry out of the Butte mines where I had dug ore. That verse written about miners and engineers and shift bosses and mule skinners and mine hoists and engines and compressors might have novelty, vigor and interest.

I had done such things for the *Inter-Mountain*, but I had thought of them as local stuff—and had continued, out in Butte, to write stuff in Bowery dialect (which I had never heard) and in English accent (with which I was not familiar) and about people and places which I knew chiefly from reading. I was writing about writing instead of about life.

The realization that the material which supplied my news stories would also supply subjects for my literature, gave a new impetus and vim to my evenings of creative work. I was still shooting in the dark so far as definite markets were concerned, but I was no longer groping in a fog for my definite inspiration.

Thus came "Songs of a Mining Camp." Ten of them. Written as I had time, during the summer of 1909. Sometime in October, 1909, I completed this sheaf of ballads, copied them, and sent them, with a modest note, to the *Saturday Evening Post*. AND THE *Post* BOUGHT THEM ALL. . . .

The sale of "Mining Camp Ballads" to the *Post* gave me a conviction of arrival. I was a *real author*, now.

Here were *ten poems—count 'em—ten!*—sold at one crack to the market of markets, to the biggest and most successful of popular publications. . . . I would go to New York where I could walk into editorial offices and lay my verses on the editor's desk instead of waiting about a week for the mails, and I'd knock the cock-eyed world for a loop.

... Though I'm ordinarily no reckless plunger, and often I'm timorous and trepid, every once in a while I give prudence what is elegantly known as the "bum's rush," and with a shout of "Gangway, please!" dive through the crowd about the table and toss my roll on a single number. This was one of those times. . . .

"So-o-o," as Ed Wynn says, my mother, my dog and I, rolled eastward on the North Coast Limited. . . .

"Give the Kid a Chance"—II

I learned from that first sketch for *Hampton's* how easily some men are defeated. And how often "ruthless and cruel New York" gets the blame for some weakling's lack of ordinary persistence and stamina. The subject of that sketch was just bursting to talk—but he wanted to be coaxed a little. The other chap had wilted at the first "No." I coaxed a little, and flattered a little, and the difficult subject spouted information from every pore. He gave me enough material for a three-volume life. But that bird who quit probably went home and told his pitying friends that he didn't have a chance, he was given an impossible assignment.

New York gets its hard-boiled and hard-hearted reputation from two kinds of people—failures and tourists. The failures return home and blame New York for their own incapacity. More people try to buck New York than any other city, hence there are more failures to paint it dark.

More tourists visit New York and see New York as a city of waiters, box office clerks and other members of the get-the-money gang, than visit any other city. And they come home to describe the Broadway spending machine as evidence of Gotham's greed, graft and avarice. The successes and the residents of New York learn to love it as kindly and generous, but they don't get back home often enough to counteract the other sort of propaganda. So Manhattan's reputation is cruel and harsh, which isn't the fact at all.

Not least, physically and intellectually, of the give-the-kid-a-chance editors in New York was William A. Johnston—"Fat Bill" Johnston—of the New York *World*. . . .

For Bill always had leisure to see the aspiring young writer. Bill didn't regard it as a waste of time to listen to the hopes and ambitions of beginners or would-be beginners. He saw them all.

"It's my job," said Bill. "Forty-nine out of fifty aspirants have nothing. But it's no waste of time to see them, for the fiftieth pays for the hours spent with the others and leaves the *World* a profit. And what does this time I devote to them amount to? About two hours a working day. An editor who says he hasn't time to see aspirants is like a purchasing agent who says he hasn't time to see salesmen. I'm as busy as other editors—which means that, counting the two hours a day devoted to seeing everybody, I put in approximately a five-hour day. The chief difference between my situation and that of other editors is that I don't bluff about it."

The result was that Bill got authors young, and he got them cheap. He bought stories for fifty dollars from authors who in a few years could command five hundred and a thousand. But because he'd been accessible and kind and because, even at fifty dollars, he was paying well as newspaper rates go, those authors were grateful. In their thousand dollar days, Bill could still have a story for fifty if he needed it.

"*Formula in Art*"

Perriton Maxwell gave me a slightly different sort of chance. Also he furnished me the most valuable technical hint I'd had since Tom Hood taught me verse forms.

Said Maxwell, "So you're a poet? Are you an inspirational poet, or can you work to order?"

"I can work to order."

"Well, here's a picture. Write me twelve lines to go with it. If they're satisfactory, I'll give you twelve dollars for them."

I came back the next day with the verses.

"Good, as a whole," he commented. "But they need a punch, or a whip, or a twist at the end to sum 'em up! Put that in and I'll buy 'em!"

I took them home and put in a twist. He bought them.

But the importance of the transaction for me was in the change he'd suggested. Why hadn't somebody told me before? Why had I been such a sap as not to see it myself without somebody telling me? Fool, dolt, idiot! You put a climax in a story—and, of course, if you weren't a total nit-wit, you'd put a climax in a poem.

When I began studying carefully the stuff I'd sold and that which I didn't seem able to sell, I found the rejected verse *always* lacked whip. It might as well stop with one stanza as three. It might be clever versification, but it hadn't any clinching power at the finish. So now I had the formula!

I owe it to Perriton Maxwell, with all thanks and the most fervent gratitude.

Critics and other amateur students of the literary craft are scornful of formula in art. But they might as justly be contemptuous of "form" in athletics. They're the same thing. The crawl, for instance, is an almost completely artificial stroke. Yet this highly mechanical "formula" has speeded up swimming incredibly. Many buxom lassies have more "power" in their limbs than Helene Madison, but they don't go through the water so fast because they haven't her perfection of form.

Yes, "heart" and "will to win" and the super-spark called "genius" are part of the equipment of a champion, but they won't make him a champion without form. The long years Tilden spent batting balls against a wall with a white line across it may not have given him the drive behind those ungettable aces of his, but those years taught him to keep the aces inside the service lines.

There are no "naturals." Some people acquire form more quickly and more "naturally" than others, that's all. Study of the career of any champion in *any* line, or of any "rated" player, for that matter, will inevitably reveal similitudes to Tilden's wall-hitting. That goes for Tunney or Dempsey, for Babe Ruth or Mathewson, for Hoover or Roosevelt.

Form!

What is it but the application of the mind to achieving the greatest results with the least energy? A formula for producing what you want to produce with the highest efficiency. You can't escape it whether you like it or not. There is a form and a formula for everything, even for formlessness—as you'll discover if you want to waste time studying vorticists, imagists, da-da -ists and ga-ga -ists.

The formula or "trick" if you prefer, that Perriton Maxwell pointed out to me, was an artifice that had been employed by every poet and versifier from Homer to Hodgson. Yet it might be called a natural artifice, because it is human nature to demand a climax to suspense. People are willing to wait for a firecracker to explode, but they're cheated if it fizzles.

"I Met Jack London at the Rand School. . . ."

. . . Neither very big, nor in the least burly, he was none the less completely, electrically masculine. His body was as sleekly, elastically powerful as that of a panther, and he walked like one.

His hands were small, but his firm handshake carried an impulse of quick power behind it. Not the hairy troglodyte, but the finely trained welter-weight. His voice was not deep, but flexible and tingling with the man's vitality. His smile was not merely a flexing of muscles, but a lighting of every feature and a flash and glimmer of warm and glowing eyes.

I loved Jack London from the moment I touched his hand. I was to see him only a few times after that dinner, and then for brief moments, yet his early death a few years later left a sense of personal loss greater than the passing of far more familiar friends.

London could talk economics, philosophy, and literature with the most erudite and intellectual of people—and enjoy every moment of it, but he would pass up a gathering of the most lofty and brilliant minds at any time to see a good prize fight, and he'd leave any assemblage of philosophers to join a poker game.

He did so on the evening of this Rand School Dinner. With that still lingering awe I possessed for all eminence, I had diffidently suggested that there was to be a modest poker game for negligible stakes at my flat, that evening, and if he cared to drop in, we'd admire to have him. His eyes lighted at the suggestion—

"Say, I'd love it," he said. "But I'm down for a high-brow confab and I've got to go. Sorry!"

So that was that, I thought. But at midnight, Jack London rang the bell at my apartment.

"Game still going?" he asked, when I opened the door. "I'm just honing for smoke and swear words and the clink of chips."

So he sat in, and was simply one of the gang, and played as hard at quarter limit as if there were no ceiling, and told us stories of South Sea and Alaskan poker games, and won most of our money, and had hamburgers with us at the corner lunch-stand at four A.M.

For all Jack's vibrant masculinity, his direct and vivid speech, his emanation of strength and vitality—the word that best describes his appeal is a feminine one—"sweet." There was a naïve, boyish and simple sweetness about Jack that was immeasurably his greatest charm.

Aside from his personal qualities, I admired in London his ability as a story-teller, and his sane refusal to let his propagandist feelings interfere with it. He wrote half a dozen propagandist books, so intended and so executed. And they were invaluable and powerful influences on the thought of his day.

But he never confused his "literary freedom" with the job in hand. If an editor wanted from Jack an adventure story, he got from Jack an adventure story, and Jack didn't feel stultified or prostituted by the fact that he wasn't doing a socialistic argument. He simply did the work before him to the best of his power, and that best was tremendously good, and he saw to it that a capitalistic press paid him the best prices going. And because he stuck to his job, he built up a prestige and power which made his definite propagandist books effective, aside from their own merit, because Jack London wrote them.

This ability to differentiate between his jobs and his opinions made Jack London, it seems to me, far freer than such free souls as Art Young, Jack Reed or Boardman Robinson.

"Berton Braley's Daily Poem"

It was at a party that I met Richard Lloyd Jones, editor of the *Wisconsin State Journal*. Jones had seen my verse and liked it. Liked it well enough to be willing to spend money to get it.

"I'd like to have a poem a day in the *Journal*," he said, "but all I can afford is ten dollars a week. And you can't afford to work for that. But Colver, of the N.E.A., is a friend of mine. I think I might be able to induce him to pay ten dollars a week for a daily poem. Thus you'd be getting twenty—with a chance for more— Want to try it?"

"What's the N.E.A.?" I asked.

"Newspaper Enterprise Association. It's a syndicate run by the Scripps-McRae outfit. Serves several hundred papers with features, pictures, and so forth."

"All right," I said.

Thus began Berton Braley's "Daily Poem," which was to run in several hundred daily papers regularly for nearly three years, first with Dick Jones paying half of my twenty a week and using the poem as part of the service, then with Colver of the N.E.A., (a prince and a great newspaperman, by the way) taking over the whole twenty a week and gradually increasing it until I was getting forty.

No, not big money, but what an audience! And what a tonic to my activity!

Newspaper readers of a daily feature get the habit of it early, and remain loyal to it long. Three years after I had ceased to work for N.E.A., I made a tour of the country and every editor of every paper in which my stuff had appeared played me up—not as a magazine poet or book writer—but as a former contributor to their feature service. Rather pleasant loyalty, that.

As to the tonic effect of this daily grind—here's more theory and practice about the literary craft. In my experience, the most important factor in productive capacity is momentum. If you git goin' you keep goin'. With six verses a week that *have* to be done, you are in the swing of it, and it is easy to take more work "in your stride." If you have no such head of pressure pushing against your brain-turbine, it is harder to start and harder to keep running. Just as starting a motor car takes more power and is more strain on the gears than accelerating in high.

It usually required me not more than two days to get out my six verses. I don't believe they would have been better if it took me two weeks, and I doubt if they'd have been as good. Besides which I would not have held my job. Don't think I'm apologizing for haste. It is my settled and to a large extent provable conviction that the best work is done the most swiftly and easily. Jobs done with sweat and blood smell of them. And when a writer boasts of how he perspired and toiled in agony over a job, he's probably trying to impress a critic. Few critics know anything whatever about the mechanics of writing. If they did, they'd be writers and not critics.

But of course there is a limit to speed. There is a legend in the Chicago office of the N.E.A. about the Berton Braley poems that I am forced to explode. The story is that I came into the office, sat down to the typewriter, and in half an hour pounded out a week's supply of verse. De Alton Valentine, the artist, who was one of the staff there, spread this tale afar. It was quite true. What Val didn't know was that I had already written those verses, and lost them on the way down to the office. But they were pretty fresh in my mind, and my stunt was mere memory and not celerity. Anybody could *type* approximately one hundred and fifty lines of verse in a half hour.

"I Had Proposed to an Average of a Girl a Year..."

With the N.E.A. job tucked in my portfolio, and no other definite prospects, I started back to New York, pausing long enough in Chicago to get engaged to a girl. Up to this time my "love life" had not been marked by success. I had proposed to an average of a girl a year for six years and had been as regularly turned down. Another proposal was coming on and this girl happened to be in the way, so she got it. Much to my amazement and embarrassment, she accepted me. This threatened to upset all my plans, but I invented an absolutely vital appointment in New York and took the next train.

For several months I wrote what I thought were perfect examples of passionate love letters, but the girl didn't. She complained of their lack of sincerity. She doubted that I loved her. I doubted it myself.

Before long her own letters began to lack fire. Mention of another man crept into them. I pretended jealousy. I almost convinced myself. After six months I hopped the train to Chicago, ostensibly to see the girl, actually to give the other man what is academically known as the "o.o." I liked him. He was obviously mad about the girl—she about him. But she didn't want to hurt me.

I got the man aside. I said:

"Jack, I'm worried. I'm fond of Nell, terrifically fond of her, but I don't want to marry her. Our engagement was a terrible mistake. Yet I don't want to hurt her. What can I do?"

"Berton," he said solemnly, "I'll confess to you. I love her myself. I think she loves me. But I was held back by Honor. Now I can speak. Thank you for being so straight with me."

I pretended to be amazed at this revelation of his love—which had been written all over him every moment he was with Nell or near her—and gave him my blessing. So all was jake, and I have no better friends in the world than this ideally happy and perfectly mated pair. But despite all denials, I believe they believe to this day that instead of a buck passer I was a noble soul renouncing Nell to the "man she loved" at whatever cost to my aching heart.

I went back to New York emitting shrill shrieks of joyous relief, and with this load off my conscience, and my health excellent, I began for the first time really to appreciate and love New York.

"The Sky's the Limit"

I am trusting to my slightly inchoate memory to depict the city in that period from 1911 to the Great War. It was cleaner than it is now, it was cheaper to live in. My mother and I had a ten-room elevator apartment overlooking Union Square, for which I paid eighty-five dollars a month. Even in these deflated days—if they are still deflated when this is read—a seventy-five cent table d'hôte can't touch the kind we got for fifty in 1911. My swellest custom-made suit was forty dollars and one I had made for fifteen dollars wasn't bad at all.

New York's skyline was that of a few lone peaks rising from a huddle of low foot-hills, instead of groups of mountain ranges with many Matterhorns outsoaring the rest. The Woolworth Building was, as I recall, in the excavation stage. The Metropolitan's seven-hundred-foot tower dominated the town's mid-section, dwarfing the Flatiron's twenty-story prow that parted the traffic—and still parts it—at Broadway and Fifth Avenue. The Times and the Heidelburg Buildings at Broadway and Forty-second Street were the Alps of the Rialto, while the Singer, the Municipal Building, the Post and the Park Row Buildings out-towered the rest of lower Manhattan.

Today, there are fourteen skyscrapers taller than the Metropolitan tower, twenty-nine higher than the Singer, six out-topping the Woolworth, and craggy blocks and ranges of hotels, lofts and office structures that leave the Times, the Flatiron [and] the Park Row merely knee-high.

Am I sighing over lost grandeurs? Not I. Nor shaking my head over the white elephants of steel and stone or fabricated material that loom so emptily just now. Aye, they've wrecked amany fortunes, they were sometimes the structures of greed rather than vision, but ten years from now, we'll again be singing panegyrics to the daring and the imagination of the men who thrust them to the blue, even if they went in the red doing it. In the long run the sky's the limit in New York—and there is a lot of sky!

"Pulps" & "Hacks"

For the lay reader—and most readers are "lay"—a definition of "pulpwood magazines" is indicated.

Actually all but the very finest of bond papers are made from wood pulp, and not from rags. But "pulp" is the trade name for the rough, unglazed stuff used for daily journals and for the unillustrated magazines. Hence "pulps."

The pulps are generally issued on a "manufacturing basis," which means that their publishers can make a profit, if circulation is adequate, without a line of advertising.

Paper, ink, labor, overhead, contents and profit must—in the pulps—be covered by the price received from the newsstands and subscriptions. Advertising, if any, is so much velvet.

Because of this policy, the pulps cannot afford fancy prices for material. Twenty years ago a cent a word was standard pay to pulp-wood contributors. Today it is two cents.

An author must be prolific to flourish at a price of one hundred dollars for a five-thousand-word short story, and twelve hundred dollars for a serial. But men like Gilbert Patten, Fred Jackson and Bob Brown poured forth fiction, lively, swift-moving and enthralling fiction, at a pace that made them twenty to forty thousand dollars a year.

It wasn't so bad being a pulpwood hack.

The main trouble with that job was the tendency to sell to these sure, but not too open-handed buyers, stuff which might bring four times the money, and ten times the glory in swankier publications. This shouldn't and wouldn't be true were editors really looking as hard for new talent as they say they are. But few editors had the ordinary enterprise to read—or have read for them—the pulps, and the O. Henrys, Roches, Van Loans and Edgar Wallaces had to wait for larger recognition until they could spare a few dozen stories to throw at the "shiny mags."

Those "pulp" magazines of vigorous adventure run a high percentage of first-rate stuff. The editors of the shiny "mags" would do well to reach out for more of these pulpwood hacks instead of waiting for the hacks to batter their doors in, as is usually necessary. A hack, if the lay reader doesn't happen to know, is simply a writer who is regularly employed doing work to order—and the pulpwoods have peculiar needs which require this type of work to keep them going.

"I Gave the Panama Canal a 'Look See'"

In 1912 I gave the Panama Canal a "look see," intending to write and sell many verses about that tremendous job. I wrote the verses, and it took me two years to sell them. But the trip gave me more enthusiasm than ever over the essential romance and glamor of this mechanistic age we live in.

The Panama Canal Zone was peopled with a curious race of madmen. The frenzy ran through the veins of all the "gold roll" men instead of ordinary blood. They ate, slept, drank, talked and dreamed Canal. Steam shovel men tore into the sides of mountains with five-ton scoops to make new records of performance. Drillers thrust Ingersolls or well drills down into the rock or dirt at heretofore unimaginable speeds. Dynamiters and powder monkeys tamped down into those holes explosives in quantities hitherto incredible, and electricians exploded these charges and moved whole mountains and valleys at a time. Bargemen scooped or sucked mud out of the canal bottom and the Chagres bed so fast that their barges almost sank under their own muck, and cranemen and shovelers slapped it on trains of cars that didn't stop, but merely paused for loads. On the Gatun dam and that of Pedro Miguel and Miraflores, riveters broke riveting records and concreters broke concreting records and fillers broke filling records until the only thing to compare with was their own performance.

I believe in the capitalistic system and private profit, but nobody ever worked for private profit or for any capitalist as these men worked for the Government of the United States and the army Colonel who was bossing the job. If this is state socialism, I'm for it. Aside from my private opinion, the canal history shows that private engineers fell down and that it wasn't until Uncle Sam took full charge that the job went through.

Anyhow, it was a glorious and energizing madness to witness. I met the man who made it possible for white men to work at it, and healthy for black and brown—Colonel Gorgas. Slim, white-haired, warm-eyed and genial, he didn't look the crusader. Crusaders seldom do. But as Sanitary Engineer of the Canal, he had conducted successfully a crusade against disease and death. He had turned a plague spot into a health resort. He had purged a country, cleaned a jungle, screened, drained, cemented, sterilized and asepticized a fever-ridden people, and made the Zone and Panama City so insectless that you could sit for hours under a tropic moon in the Plaza and never scratch a bite.

Colonel Goethals was a great administrator and a great engineer. His job was as splendidly done as that of Colonel Gorgas, but without Gorgas and his "bug hunters," it couldn't have been done at all.

"The Busy Bard of Business"

This Panama experience accentuated my feeling for the lyric possibilities in men, machines and industry. I felt that people could not be too often reminded that in their humdrum routine of today, there was, if they chose to see it, more enchantment than Merlin at his mythical best could have imagined, and that the foreman of a machine-shop or the boss of a tunnel gang was living daily more real romance than Launcelot knew in a lifetime.

This was, and is, the recurrent theme of my more serious verse. I have applied it with the same genuine conviction to vacuum cleaners as to airplanes, to mechanical dishwashers as to turbine generators. I see the same high adventure in the "sandhog" shoveling dirt in an air lock, as in the engineer who projects the plans for a Holland Tunnel and calculates the meeting of its two halves to the exact inch. They're all on the job of "making the dream come true." Which is, by the way, a phrase first used by me in the "Miracle Workers," that I wore threadbare in many poems until one of my franker friends suggested that my "dreams coming true" were getting to be nightmares to him.

But it was this concern of mine with industry as a lyric theme that led Floyd Parsons, then editor of *Coal Age*, to send for me. The McGraw-Hill Company published *Coal Age, Power*, the *Engineering and Mining Journal*, the *Engineering News* and the *American Machinist*—each a trade magazine dominant in its field.

Parsons wanted verse for *Coal Age*.

He was one editor whom I didn't have to convince that people read verse. He said,

"Mr. Braley, I like your stuff—particularly what you write about machinery and men in industry. *Coal Age* is a highly technical magazine, but I think it would be very much better for an occasional, or even a regular poem about the human side of the coal business. I don't know where people get the idea that poetry isn't read. Did you ever notice that when doctors or lawyers or plumbers or boilermakers get together in conventions, they bust out into poetry—usually very bad poetry, but revealing that they want to express their enthusiasms lyrically. Did you ever note that if you're talking to a drummer or a railroad man or a business man or an undertaker and you happen to touch on his pet hobby, that he opens his wallet and takes out a dog-eared piece of newspaper or magazine verse that he's treasured because it says what he'd like to say in rhyme? Does he carry around prose editorials or essays or even paragraphs in the same manner? He does not.

"Man is a rhythmic animal and his favorite reading is rhyme. The sales of collections and anthologies of verse and the lasting popularity of Riley and Holmes and Longfellow and Kipling and—"

"Wait a minute, Mr. Parsons," I said. "You're making *my* selling talk. You needn't go on. I'll be glad to do verse for your magazine and I think it'll be fun. If we can adjust the matter of compensation—"

We adjusted that with no difficulty and for the next four or five years I was the staff poet of *Coal Age*. And the response was such that after a few months I was also the staff poet of the *American Machinist*, *Power*, and the *Engineering Journal*. Only the *Engineering News* remained unconvinced and unversified.

It was a profitable, interesting job. There were never four more dependable editors to deal with, and I had a ready market for from two to four verses a week at good rates. These men admitted they were not poetical experts and trusted to me to give them my best, and I tried to. Often this market was a life-saver when general trade was dull. . . .

I don't know how much of my work for the McGraw-Hill Company one would call poetry, but I know that there was inspiration in trying to sing in verse the bark of airdrills, the plunge and rattle of cages, the roar of the breaker, the throb and thud of reciprocating engines, the purr of dynamos, the rolling rhythm of overhead cranes, the hiss and whir of belts, the clank of punches and the shriek of reamers. With the strength, the spirit and the imagination of man amidst them.

This was what I tried for, and though on the average, all I achieved was competent verse with a mechanic slant, which editors and readers liked enough to make it a fair bargain, once in a while I knocked out a home run. And for the *American Machinist* I did what was to prove the most popular and famous of all my verses, "The Thinker."

Yet "The Thinker" was one of those "tailored to order" things that uncommercial critics condemn. Mr. Alvord, editor of the *Machinist*, asked me if I couldn't do some verses about the brains of industry—the ideal executive, the creator and planner. I thought I could.

I don't think "The Thinker" is my best piece of verse, but the world (which means the few thousand people who happen to like your stuff) appears to have decided that it is. It has been published and republished in literally thousands of newspapers, periodicals and house organs. It has been made into greeting cards and wall mottoes and desk blotters. It has been forged into iron and copper placques. A Detroit millionaire in flusher days paid me two hundred and fifty dollars for an autographed copy. A Chicago efficiency engineer paid me one hundred dollars to use it on two thousand embossed cards that he sent to his customers and prospects. (That wasn't as profitable as I thought, because in a casual moment I agreed to autograph the cards and it took me two days.) "The Thinker" is in about every modern anthology of verse that I know about—and probably several that I don't—and it still brings in one or two hundred dollars a year from textbook publishers. It also bears the acid test of plagiarism, having been chosen by at least "forty thieves" to publish in various places as their own work. Which is a most unfortunate choice for the plagiarist, because, since it was a custom-built job, I can prove by the man who ordered it that I wrote it. Which isn't always the case when you want to establish that you wrote something you wrote. . . .

As minstrel of mechanics for McGraw-Hill, I attracted the attention of various other industrial publishers, and industrialists. The editor of the *Railroad Master Mechanic* hired me to chant in rhyme a saga of master mechanics in convention assembled. He showed me some stuff he had already published which he thought was excellent. It was awful. I could have written him the most dog-eared of doggerel and he would have considered it grand. But, having a conscience, such as it is, I tried to give this rhymed story some authentic power and swing, and I think I succeeded.

Then the Mergenthaler people sent for me, and I wrote several different lays for their *Bulletin*, which was a distinguished and sumptuous example of the printing art.

For the *New York Edison Magazine* I produced a poem on the power house—a lyric of which I am still proud, and which has been reprinted almost as much as "The Thinker."

I even sold a poem to the New York Telephone Company. About the Telephone Directory—and it was published in the telephone directory!

I was also, on occasions, a troubadour for the National Tube Works, the Hyatt Roller Bearing Company, the Anaconda Copper Company, and half a dozen others.

Merle Thorpe of the *Nation's Business* thought I might possibly hit his readers' fancy with some business ballads. He seemed to be right, for the first one he published, "Business is Business," is second only to "The Thinker" in popularity with anthologists. Thorpe became one of my steadiest and best customers.

Forbes Magazine, the *Caxton* (now defunct), the *Iron Age*, and some ten or fifteen other trade journals and house organs whose names I have forgotten, ran my material.

It may be difficult for theorists about the high purpose of poetry to believe that I found inspiration in this type of work, but I did. There was a challenge to what vision and imagination I had, and to all the technique I had developed, in making these mechanical ballads something more than mechanical. I not only regard this period in my versifying as education for a career, but as very much of a career in itself, and I'd ask nothing better than to be again the busy bard of business and the merry minstrel of mechanics.

It was mere accident that started me in the greeting card line. A little verse called "Nuthin'," published in the *Woman's Home Companion*, brought a letter from a small publisher in Boston. He thought those verses might make a nice greeting card. Would I allow him to use them?

I would—for a ten per cent royalty. He wrote:

"I accept your offer, if I must, but wouldn't you rather have fifteen dollars flat?"

I stuck to my royalty idea—which was lucky. In various forms, as a greeting card, a calendar, a booklet, and a wall motto, that little silly lyric has brought me in nearly two thousand dollars, and still drops a small check into my mailbox twice a year.

Hear ye, hear ye, all authors, would-be or are—never sell anything, any time, anywhere, outright for a flat rate. The least of your bits of stone may be the corner stone of a perfectly grand temple!

"Genius Doesn't Starve"

I think some publisher must have originally have been responsible for disseminating the idea that commercial success and art don't go together. It is obvious that if a publisher can make the poet think starving in a garret is the way to immortal fame, the poet won't be sordid enough to insist on gross mercenary details like royalties. He won't be sordid enough—and in his famished condition he won't have the courage. So he'll sell his copyright for a very small mess of pottage.

But this stuff about starving genius is a lie.

Genius doesn't starve.

By and large and in the main the great ones were prophets not without honor in their own country or their own time, and not without practical pecuniary recognition, either.

Homer is a mythical figure, but none of the myths depict him as begging his bread. Anacreon must have done pretty well, thank you, to buy all the wine he sang about. Horace seems to have been well treated by Maecenas. A poet had to have a patron in those days, of course, but those whose works have descended to us, including Vergil and Ovid, appear to have found generous appreciation from the magnates of the period, and to have lived as comfortably as they required.

Dante and Petrarch appear to have had a tough time of it in their love affairs, but there is no record with which I am familiar to show that they starved for anything but love. Villon's troubles with the law were not due to the lack of popularity of his poems, but to his ruthless racketeering. As a matter of fact he sang himself out of the noose and into prosperity on numerous occasions.

Shakespeare was the George M. Cohan plus the Belasco of his time from the standpoint of box-office success. Marlowe, Herrick and Sir John Suckling did not sing to deaf ears. Sheridan and Goldsmith, Pope and Swift, earned contemporary praise and money with their pens. Balzac, Victor Hugo and Dumas were best sellers. Goethe and Schiller and Heine, were, if I am not mistaken, paid well as pay went in those days. Byron sold *Don Juan* for a sum that even today would represent fat serial and book prices. Keats had no real monetary success, but remember that he died at twenty-six, which is earlier than most authors arrive, and that—even then—his financial situation was rather due to mismanagement than to lack of popular appreciation.

We find Ibsen, Björnson and Maeterlinck enjoying ample returns from their work while they lived. We know, or should know, that Tennyson, though a rich man anyhow, commanded lucrative rates for his poems and held for scores of years not only the laureateship, but a supreme place in popular regard. Kipling's poetry alone has made him sums that represent opulence to most men.

Our own Longfellows, Holmeses, Whittiers, Emersons and Lowells were not unregarded by the populace, nor unregardful of the monetary side of their craft. Poe is an exception, if you wish, but it is my unsympathetic theory that Poe's difficulties were due rather to complete business imbecility than to popular blindness. Whitman was no outstanding financial success, but I sometimes wonder if Whitman was as outstanding a poet as the critics assume.

James Whitcomb Riley made enough money writing and reading his poems to enable him to leave his family comfortable, and one hundred thousand dollars to a college!

In fact, the only poets I can recall who bear out this general belief that genius starves in garrets are Chatterton and Milton. Chatterton actually did starve, I believe. But when we come to examine the case clinically, don't we find that he is famous rather for starving than for the lasting merit of his poems?

As for Milton, all I recall of the legend is that he sold "Paradise Lost" for ten pounds or ten dollars, I forget which. Which shows that Milton was a bad bargainer, but not that the public didn't appreciate his poem. And I believe that more exact research would reveal that Milton did much better than that with the bulk of his work.

However, conceding that these two were great and greatly neglected, the overwhelming preponderance of the evidence is that genius gets along not so badly in a rough world. And that the men whose work lives on, were mostly men who lived on their own work. . . .

And I can add that there are plenty of poets, in addition to those I have pointed out in the past, who are making a living out of their poetry *now*. If "poets include writers of good verse."

Of course, if commentaters use the *a priori* argument they can defeat this assertion. They can say that if it sells it isn't a poem. Which is unanswerable and unreasonable. . . .

Modestly eliminating myself for the nonce—which will be grateful after several hundred pages of nothing much but myself—I will name a few poets, "including good verse writers," who do make a living by their poetry: John Masefield, Alfred Noyes, Rudyard Kipling, J. C. Squire, Edwin Arlington Robinson, Stephen Benet, "Ted" Robinson, Edna St. Vincent Millay, Dorothy Parker, Robert Frost, Arthur Guiterman, Douglas Malloch, S. E. Kiser, Walt Mason,

Robert W. Service, Ogden Nash, James J. Montague, Arthur Lippman.

There are unquestionably a dozen others I don't immediately recall, but each and every one of these I have named make the equivalent of a decent, and in some cases, a lavish, living out of verse alone.

I don't intend to rate the poets in any order of merit, it would be presumptuous on my part, and anyhow they're mostly friends of mine. Hence I won't say that I can't read most of Edwin Arlington Robinson because he seems foggy and amorphous—and I will say that despite this he writes a lot of good verse I *can* read. And that two of his epics were best sellers.

There is, however, no danger in applauding the superb craftsmanship of Edna St. Vincent Millay and what seems to me her gorgeous poetic imagination. I think I can allow myself enough rope to say that Dorothy Parker's deft felicity of rhyme and phrase considerably relieves the monotony of her performance on a one-stringed harp. I've never met Ogden Nash, but when I do, I don't believe he would resent my saying to him:

"Mr. Nash, when your 'Hard Lines' first came out I was mad. Mad that I hadn't discovered your clever, but obvious trick years ago. Oh, yes, I enjoyed the stuff, doggone it, but I felt I might be taking the same mad march hares out of my own hat. But lately, Mr. Nash, you have been doing a lot of straight stuff. And the trick of it isn't obvious, and the tunes you play are varied. So are your forms and meters. I like your style, Mr. Nash."

I doubt if Arthur Guiterman, whom I have known for twenty years, would resent my opinion that while he is perhaps the most dextrous spinner of light and lilting lyrics extant, his essays into the field of vigorous adventure don't have quite the vigorous tread of lusty rovers. Though "Hills" lifts your feet and your eyes aloft.

Douglas Malloch would probably be a little irked at my opinion that his sentiment is sentimental, but perhaps his feelings would be soothed by the fact that I think his daily verses competent and workmanlike. S. E. Kiser has retired after forty years of daily verse writing, and probably doesn't care that I always found his ideas good and his execution metrically precise but a trifle heavy-footed.

Walt Mason has so few illusions about himself and his corn-fed philosophy, that he might even be flattered at my judgment, which is that in homely humor, and in whimsical handling of his gayly rippling rhymes, he is almost by himself.

Ted Robinson of the *Cleveland Plain Dealer* knows that I think him the best of the newspaper poets, and not to be snooted at in any list of clever versifiers in the contemporary prints.

Robert W. Service is mostly Kipling-and-water, but when he starts, on his own, to mush through Alaska, leaving Kipling out of his pack, he swings with the veritable sourdough swagger.

Jimmie Montague's daily topical poem in the *New York Herald-Tribune* is the best daily topical poem written, and nobody writes any better topical poems anywhere. I don't know how he hits them off the news so brilliantly, for I can read four newspapers a day, every day, and find a topic to versify not oftener than once a week.

Yes, all these bards are "good versifiers" and all of them are making a living out of verse.

"Modern" Art

One of the stories told of Harry Dart is worth preserving, I think. Harry went to a private exhibition of cubist and futurist art, backed by a wealthy woman friend of his who prided herself on modernity, and who played patroness to various young "radical" and "independent" painters.

Harry wandered glumly though the rooms, looking at the paintings with blinking eyes, and growing glummer at each glance. The patroness rushed up to him.

"Oh, Harry," she gushed, "aren't they wonderful? Aren't they splendid? Don't you love them?"

"No," said Harry.

"You don't like them?"

"No," Harry growled, "I don't and I'm damn glad of it, for if I *liked* the goddam things I'd shoot myself."

"Keep It Going"

These years from 1911 to 1915 were a most prolific period. Six verses a week for the N.E.A. and two to four for McGraw-Hill were a minimum. Besides this, I kept from twenty-five to sixty verses in the mails as a matter of routine.

Until a manuscript had made five calls, I never reëxamined it except to note the title for my card index and slip it into a new envelope for another editorial address in the next mail. After five calls, I reread it. If I found myself reluctantly agreeing with the editors that it wasn't as good as I thought when I wrote it, it went into the wastebasket, or if the idea still seemed good, it was rewritten in another manner. If, on the contrary, I found myself muttering, "Why, the blank so-and-sos, whad duh they mean by chucking this work of genius back," it continued its travels until it got dog-eared, when it was recopied and "went some more." When verses sold, I wrote new ones and replenished my stock. Results, commercially at least, justified my procedure. I came to the arrogant conclusion, which I still hold, that I knew better what the editors wanted than they knew themselves. For though nine submissions is my average to a sale, my sales average is ninety-five per cent of my product. And the total is nearly nine thousand published pieces.

That is a lot of verse. Laid line to line and end to end it would make about ten linear miles of poetic feet. But the travel necessary to place that ten miles of verse in print reaches almost astronomical figures. While the greater part of it caromed or ricocheted back and forth in the New York area where most publications have their head-quarters, a great deal of it shot out to Detroit, Cleveland, Chicago, Philadelphia, Dallas, Elgin, Kansas City and San Francisco.

Hence five hundred miles is certainly a modest estimate of the distance covered by my average manuscript before it found a buyer. Which brings my manuscript mileage up to five million. That would take one manuscript ten times to the moon and back—and if there were magazines published in the moon I would probably have sub-mitted some on the first rocket. . . .

With this general system of persistency I combined an individually directed attack on certain publications. These certain publications resisted my persistent attack as stubbornly as I pressed it. But so long as there remained a market that hadn't published something of mine, I was obdurately resolved to make my appearance in its pages. In several cases, this wouldn't mean any special kudos or financial profit, but it would enable me to assert that I had "made 'em all."

Harper's courteously rejected everything for five years and then capitulated on one piece of verse. The *Century* held out for a decade, and then Mr. Johnson, his powers of resistance a little weakened with time, bought a humorous nautical ballad. *Harper's Bazaar*, under two or three different editors and owners, sent me nothing more encouraging than a rejection slip for eighteen years, until Charlie Towne commissioned me to versify a set of Fish's pictures. *Scribner's* stood siege for twelve years before I breached the wall with a love lyric. The *Atlantic* returned my first contribution offered in 1904. It continued that policy with calm Boston determination—and with no more encouragement than I might read in the printed slips accompanying the manuscripts—until 1932, when three of the shells sent over in that twenty-eight-year bombardment, cracked the citadel and exploded in the magazine.

In the case of *Adventure*, Arthur Hoffman's magazine, the wall to knock down was not built against me alone, but to shut out all poets. Hoffman thought verse had no place in his kind of publication.

But Arthur Hoffman, while definite in his views, was by no means "sot." And since I had just as definite an idea that verse—well, my verse anyhow—should have a place in his magazine, I wrote some ballads I hoped might demonstrate my point.

Hoffman listened to my arguments on the universality of rhythmic appeal, and considered my assertion that he was hamstringing his magazine by omitting verse. Then he read my samples.

"I guess you're right, Berton," he said. "I'll take one of these. And tell the other rhymesters the taboo on verse is off."

It was so completely "off" that *Adventure* became one of the best of markets for verse, and four years later broke all magazine traditions in America by printing twenty-four pages of it in one lump—a thousand-and-one-line ballad called "Tales of the Hot Dog Tavern," and written, oddly enough, by the modest hero of these here now reminiscences.

But with all due credit to Arthur Hoffman's final acceptance of that long poem—which went very well with the readers, as it happens—it took me four years of reiterated resubmission of the manuscript before even the open-minded Hoffman opened his pages to my opus.

One fortress is still impregnable. The ramparts of *Vanity Fair* remain unscaled, though perhaps I might claim to have entered its keep through a congratulatory letter of mine to George Jean Nathan, which was published in the correspondence department.

Or I might get credit for an assist on the ground that that same Mr. Nathan once quoted my 'Nathan, Mencken and God' in a *Vanity Fair* article. But in my own records I count as hits only those shots which result in tribute from the treasury. In other words, stuff bought and paid for.

However, insurance tables give me twenty years' expectation of life, and I may yet upset the No Braley tradition of *Vanity Fair*. If and when I succeed, I shall cease to be greatly concerned with subsequent sales. All I want is to make my list complete, for with the exception of *Vanity Fair*, I've now "made 'em all" so far as I can remember.

The reward in conquering these difficult markets is purely moral. If I had never made a sale to any of them, my income would not have suffered, nor such value as my name may possess have been enhanced. The easier and more receptive markets were better pay and better publicity, and it was only me bloody pride and pertinacity that got a satisfaction out of being the irresistible force that moves the immovable body.

If all this sounds like factory language, it *is* factory language. Every author is a factory, producing literary wares. Producing them may be art, but selling them is business. Each author follows the method that succeeds for him, or that suits him best. And if he's frank, he'll admit that art hasn't anything to do with that phase of it. I'm neither boosting nor deprecating my method, but I think it is worth setting down.

Basically, the motif is that same nagging persistence with which I was born, and which makes me unable to believe that, even after the seventy-fifth rejection, something I regard as worthy of publication can't be sold. And having sold not one but several manuscripts to the seventy-seventh and the eighty-sixth publication to which it was submitted, I continue to cherish fond hopes in a few old-timers that are on their second century of rejections. It isn't that I don't quit, but that I can't.

At this juncture I offer my advice to the young author. It's old stuff, but sound. "If you believe in your work, keep it going!"

"The Adventurers' Club"

The Adventurers' Club waned after a few years because it became increasingly apparent that real adventurers wouldn't come, or couldn't talk interestingly when they did come, or if they were capable of making their adventures interesting in speech, usually got too drunk to talk. The club came to be a sort of forum for writers of adventure stories, and there was much more discussion of the hunting of tame checks than of wild animals. . . .

The best speech ever made at the Adventurers' was by Stefansson. It was in the early years of the war.

"I don't think I belong in an Adventurers' Club," he said. "It has been my experience as an explorer, that an adventure is a mistake, and represents a failure in preparation. If you plan your expedition properly, you don't have adventures. Any 'adventures' I have I apologize for. They've either been due to my own lack of knowledge or to somebody's failing to obey orders. I wouldn't care to boast about my displays of ignorance or my failure at organization.

"I talked with an Italian who had laid nearly all the mine barrages for the Allies. I said, 'You must be a very brave man.'

"He said, 'No, I am timid. Therefore I am alive. The brave men in my organization—they are all blown to pieces. Because I am timid, you see, I am afraid of a mine. Because I am afraid of a mine, I am very careful with it. If you are very careful with a mine, it does not explode until it is intended to explode. So I live—the brave, careless men, they die.' "

"Songs of the Workaday World"

[Nineteen-fifteen] was a sort of epochal autumn for me, anyhow. I was married, I went on the peace trip, my first book of collected poems, "Songs of the Workaday World," was published,—and I made Who's Who. The marriage didn't last, the peace trip was a nightmare, the book was only a moderate success, and getting into Who's Who has had no effect upon my fortunes except to put me on every sucker list in the country. But they all had their thrill for a space, and you can't ask much more of life than that.

Sinclair Lewis was responsible for my book. I had been peddling it hither and yon for a year or more, getting nice letters but no results, until Lewis, then a reader for George Doran, read it, liked it, and went to the bat for me. Doran wouldn't undertake it except on an agreement that there were to be no royalties unless at least a thousand copies were sold. I gambled with him on that.

Lewis wrote the "blurb" on the jacket:

"The rhymes of a real man's man. They swing like a racing car rounding a curve, they gladden the heart like the meadow lark's note on the first morning of a vacation.

"Songs of sailors and miners and cowpunchers, of muckers and trainmen and of all the ordinary people who wear boots and get the world's work done.

"For the wanderer here are memories of his most wonderful hikes. For the restless stay-at-homes here are invitations to the open road. With this book, Mr. Braley becomes the one American poet for men and women who love fresh air too much to stay indoors and read any ordinary verse.

"Yet the bookworm will be stirred by the melody, the rhythm, the art of these songs."

"Red" meant all that, too. I think he lyricized what I was trying to do rather than what I succeeded in doing, but that blurb so flattered my fancy that after seventeen years I can quote it verbatim, which I can't do with any of the verses in "Songs of the Workaday World," or any other of my ten books of verse. Several critics suggested that the best part of the book was the blurb on the jacket.

The combination of what Lewis put on the outside and I put inside the volume sold the thousand copies inside a month, and led to a contract for three more volumes, none of which—as is often the way in that adventure called publishing—came anywhere near the four or five thousand sale of the "Workaday World."

In common with nineteen out of twenty authors, I've never had a best seller. But I've only had two complete "flops," which is uncommon. The wise writer doesn't count his chickens until they are hatched, knowing well that his book is likely to lay an egg, a metaphor so mixed that you can call it an omelette. The only practical way to view the publishing gamble is to get the best serial price possible, and figure the book rights as so much velvet even if the nap is thin.

When you realize that the average book sale is fifteen hundred copies, that is the way to bet—not on fifty thousand.

"Money is a Measure of Labor and Time"

There is a seventy-five-thousand-word manuscript in my desk which touches a few high and low spots on my world trip. It's unsold. Aside from that manuscript and sundry verses that did sell, all I got out of my circumnavigatory tour was a permanent infection in my feet that ended my handball playing, and a conviction that the provincial American who thinks we do things better at home is perfectly right.

So, since I promised the reader to "step on it," the general purport of that seventy-five thousand words was that I admired the Japanese and didn't like them, and liked the Chinese and didn't admire them. That in the main the "mysterious East" seemed to be filthy and full of fleas, and the ancient oriental philosophy under which four hundred and fifty million coolies were miserable so that four hundred and fifty thousand mandarins and tycoons could be luxurious, didn't appeal to my crass materialistic brain as being so hot. . . .

But the trip netted me one more grand guy to add to my list. This was Bartlett Thane. Geologist, engineer, captain of industry, multimillionaire, good fellow, golden talker about the world of men in geological terms, sourdough in Alaska, engineer and geologist all over the world. Able to narrate his own adventures entrancingly, and ever entranced with the other man's adventures that differ from his own.

Thane had never met a professional writer before. He eviscerated me of everything I knew about the writing business and added it to his store of general knowledge and information. A grand guy. Incidentally I have met a dozen or so captains of industry. And they were all unusual men and unusually good companions. I hear much talk among writers and artists of the stupidity of the business man and the industrial tycoon—but I know more bores who are intellectuals.

Even sergeants of industry, or corporals of trade, are not so dumb if you happen to hit the pitch on your tuning fork to which they vibrate. . . .

But to recur to my Captain of Industry. It was at Nikko that, after we reached the top of the hill of ascending temples, glittering with red, gold and black lacquer, Thane said:

"Braley, what do you suppose those temples would have cost to build with American labor, today?"

156

"Oh, Bart, how gross!" exclaimed his wife.

"And how very American!" I jibed—merely to hear what he would say.

Thane snorted.

"I know," he said. "And somebody ought to be around to quote Oscar Wilde at me, 'Americans know the cost of everything and the value of nothing.' Well, I know the value of that epigram—it's nothing. Just a smart crack.

"I wonder what those temples cost because money is a measure of labor and time—the best and most accurate measure we have.

"If Oscar Wilde didn't figure his royalties in money, what did he figure them in? If I could estimate what it would cost in American money with American craftsmen to reproduce those temples, I'd have a picture of what they represent in human energy, thought and imagination that I could get in no other way. I could translate the job of the old Japanese builders and workers into my own language and the temples would mean a hundred times more to me. If you know what a thing cost you know its value and that's been true since the first two anthropoid apes swiped coconuts."

So Thane and I figured that the reproduction cost would be about three hundred million dollars, or half what it cost to build the Panama Canal—and Nikko is no longer to me a mere picture post card of shrines, but a vast achievement of beauty, brains and labor. I like it better that way.

In Defense of "My Great God Kipling"

There was a near dramatic meeting at the Daytons' between Harry Kemp and myself. It was back "befoah the wah." Possibly a year previous to our encounter, Harry had written a brief and virulent attack on my Great God Kipling.

But let the United Press, which put the controversy on the wire, furnish the details:

"By United Press Leased Wire.

"New York, Jan. 10 (1914). — Petulant, apparently, because England jailed him when he arrived on her chalk cliffs a penniless stowaway, Harry Kemp, the hatless long-haired Kansas rhymester, took a bitter fling at Rudyard Kipling as a poet.

"Berton Braley today took up the cudgel for the creator of 'Mulvaney,' and thus brought on a poetry duel . . .

"Kemp wrote this:

'To Kipling:

> 'Vile singer of the bloody deeds of empire,
>   And of the bravery that exploits the poor,
> Exalter of subservience to masters,
>   Bard of the race that bound and robbed the Boer—
> We note your metaphors that shine and glisten
>   But underneath your sounding verse we see
> The exploitation and the wide corruption,
>   The lying and the vice and misery.
> Your people lay upon the backs of others—
>   The bullet and the prison and the rod,
> Wherewith ye scourge the races that subserve you
>   And then blaspheme by blaming it on God.'

"To which Braley promptly replied:

'To Harry Kemp:

> 'Emitter of unnecessary noises,
>   Blowing a penny whistle loud and long,
> Trying to drown the blaring of the trumpets
>   With puny tootlings or with futile song,
> We hear your notes of thin and strident clamor;
>   We see you whirl in wild and dervish glee,
> Shrilling at Kipling—and we look upon you
>   Saying in wonder "ooinellishe"?
> Not always does the master sing his noblest;
>   Sometimes he carols in a dreary style,
> But who are you—you cheap and tawdry bardlet—
>   To hint him servile or to call him "vile." ' "

There was quite a party at the Daytons' that evening, and when Harry Kemp, six feet and one hundred and eighty-five pounds of masculinity, strode into the studio, Helena sidled over to me with the gentle hope of slipping me out before Harry and I collided.

But some impulsive enthusiast who hadn't heard of the controversy, shrilled, "Ooh! These two poets must meet each other" and led the burly Harry toward me. An apprehensive silence fell as the enthusiast made the introduction.

But Harry grabbed my hand in his powerful fist and bellowed:

"Berton Braley, eh! Well, I'm sure glad to know you. You gave me the God-damndest best lacing I ever got in print—and I had it coming. I can quote the whole thing to you, boy, if you want to know what I think of it. 'Cheap and tawdry bardlet'—you said it. That's what I was when I wrote that tripe. But I've been around a lot since I wrote that, and I'm not so cocksure of my radical opinions any more—and let's have a drink to Rudyard Kipling!"

So we had a drink to Rudyard Kipling, and Harry Kemp and I were friends. . . .

Braley at Fifty

Even at fifty I hate to leave before the party's over. If it is a good party I don't want to miss any of it, if it is a dull party there is always the chance that something may happen to make it good. And if that doesn't happen, you might gather a few indefatigable souls together out of the guest list and organize "something else again" to save the evening. When I shall cease to feel that way about parties I shall know "it won't be long now" and arrange my affairs accordingly.

I enjoy almost any kind of a game, and I like any kind of reading matter, high- or low-brow, which seems to me competently done and interesting. Which leaves me cold to Joyce's "Ulysses" and lost in the fog of Proust and the later Henry James.

Mentally I am hard to depress and quick to resurge. Physically I seem to be sound, and philosophically I am a pragmatist and believe that any system that works is a good system, bad as it may be, and that capitalism does the job of feeding, housing and clothing people—at its worst—better than any other system that has been tried. I believe in the Revolution, just as sincerely as any communist, but I think it is a gradual and not violent change that grows out of normal conditions as well as out of world depressions such as we've known since 1929.

I have fewer general enthusiasms and prejudices than I had at twenty-five, but my specific ones haven't cooled. I think liquor is a social, political and economic liability, I believe that national prohibition was more of a success than any other system of control was or ever will be; I think the logic of events will make us go back to it—and I like to drink and occasionally get drunk. I like my heroes and don't like debunkers. I hate poverty, injustice, greed and war, and don't know what we're going to do about any of them. But I have hopes.

If I find somebody is treading on my heels and I'm treading on those of the man ahead of me, I figure maybe I'm out of step with the regiment, and not the regiment with me. So I listen for the drum beat. I'm conventional because it's simpler to be so, and when it isn't simpler, I'm unconventional.

This could go on for several hundred pages, but the sum of it is that at fifty, so far as I'm able to detect myself, I feel and act and react very much as I did anywhere north of thirty-five. If this seems the myopic observation of complacent middle age, maybe so—but that myopia extends to my friends and acquaintances.

There must be something youth-preserving in the uncertainty, precariousness or what you will of free lancing, for by and large the artists and writers whom I have known for twenty years seem to me to age imperceptibly, if at all, and to approach or pass fifty with no more rheumatic twinges than they had at thirty. Springy of step, bright of eye, resilient and elastic of mind, they step out blithely along another long row of mileposts.

At fifty I am a little weary of financial uncertainty, but I still like my job, because, as I said before, nobody but myself can take it away from me. I like it because the "free" in free lancing means *free*. Because, within the normal limits of human liberty, I have been free to live where I chose, do as I chose, with neither time clock nor boss to fix my goings and comings.

I like it because it has taken me over a great deal of the world and made me acquainted with a great many people. I like it because it has taught me that most of those people are a decent lot, and the grand guys among them outnumber the mean birds by six or eight to one. Maybe I have been fortunate, but in looking back over the years which I remember, I can recall no friend who has been treacherous, and hundreds of strangers who have been friends. I have had a lot of fun, some tragedy, and one serious purpose in life—to carol and chronicle as best I can, the romance, the adventure, the gallantry and the everlasting courage of that fallible, stupid, fumbling and indomitable biped—Man!

STEP LIVELY, PLEASE

I am old as the hills
   And there's snow on my crest,
But the heart of me thrills
   With an unageing zest
At blithe Youth, elate
   With old dreams and new laughter,
And at men fighting Fate
   For the goals they are after.

I am old, but the light
   In my eyes is on duty
To capture the bright
   Glowing magic of beauty.
My old pulses hammer
   My old fibres dance
In rhythm with glamor
   In tune with romance.

I'm ancient, but never,
   I swear, shall I fail
To make new endeavor
   Or break a new trail,
Find joy in new skills
   With new courage to prime them.
I am old as the hills
   But I still dare to climb them.

LIVE PERFORMANCE OF BRALEY POETRY

Linda Tania Abrams presents dramatic readings of Berton Braley's poetry and prose for audiences around the U.S. and Europe.

Audiences have commented:

"We all enjoyed it tremendously...Linda Abrams' performance was worthy of Braley's poetry. Her delivery was full of energy and enthusiasm, yet she also managed to capture the solemn reverence and wit..."

— Betsy Speicher, President, SCOA

"...a real and uplifting treat, a positive shot in the arm..."

— Bruce Evoy, Lecturer,
University of Toronto (ret.)

"Linda's presentation makes these poems come alive. Linda is a very talented actress...She infuses the poems with strength and sensitivity. It is truly a joy to see her perform."

— Yaron Brook, HCOA

Linda Tania Abrams is the creator and Director of *Past Times with Good Company*, a "living history" performance troupe which makes the people of various time periods "come alive." Based in Los Angeles, they have completed three performing tours of Britain, in addition to local work. Formerly a constitutional attorney, Ms. Abrams left active law practice in the mid-'80s to pursue interests in history, the performing arts, and restoration of old buildings.

For more information, please contact:

Linda Tania Abrams
856 N. Harper Avenue   or
Los Angeles, CA 90046

The Atlantean Press
354 Tramway Drive
Milpitas, CA 95035